praise for
Jan Johnsen & The Spirit of Stone

~⌇

"Jan Johnsen successfully conveys the poetic qualities of stone through insightful observations, descriptive examples and, more importantly, with practical advice for novice and professional garden designers."

~ **Richard Alomar,** RLA, ASLA, Department of Landscape Architecture, Rutgers University

"The Spirit of Stone is an insightful look into the many ways of using natural stone in a garden. Jan's crisp descriptions and wonderful photographs open our eyes to the unique addition of this material – in all its forms – into landscapes."

~ **Bill Thomas,** Executive Director, Chanticleer Garden, author of *The Art of Gardening*

"In the same loving and passionate spirit with which she brought garden and design lovers *Heaven is a Garden*, Jan Johnsen now brings us *The Spirit of Stone*. This book provides insights and photos of every possible way to use stone in your garden: as accents, as art, as walls, as drainage, as steps, with plants or for paths."

~ **Jim Peterson,** Publisher, *Garden Design* magazine

"Jan Johnsen's intimate relationship with stone, honed over a long design career, shines through every page of this practical guide to using stone in residential gardens. Perhaps more importantly, she explains why this most elemental of materials creates a timeless sensuality that no other garden material can."

~ **Carolyn Mullet,** designer; on Facebook: "Garden Design by Carolyn Mullet"

"*The Spirit of Stone* focuses in on the soulfulness, authenticity, beauty and practicality of stonework in an outdoor setting. …a delightful celebration of the versatility of this solid, durable natural element."

~ **Fran Sorin,** author of *Digging Deep: Unearthing Your Creative Roots Through Gardening*

"Jan's great love for the art of gardening and enthusiasm for great stone work is apparent on every page. *The Spirit of Stone* is a great resource for inspiration in the garden."

~ **Devin Devine,** stone artist, mason – Devine Escapes

"Celebrated garden author and landscape designer Jan Johnsen has distilled her sophisticated natural stone expertise into a clearly written, companionable guide to stone gardening success. I predict *The Spirit of Stone* will be treasured by beginners and garden experts alike."

~ **Miriam Goldberger,** author of *Taming Wildflowers*

"Jan Johnsen leaves no stone unturned in introducing readers to the wonderful world of masonry. Her marriage of hardscape and horticulture assures *The Spirit of Stone* rock-star status on your gardening bookshelf."

~ **David Beaulieu,** landscaping expert for About.com

"*The Spirit of Stone* is an elegant paean to the use of stone in the garden. Jan Johnsen explores the rich traditions in using stone by artists and craftsmen through the age, and provides helpful suggestions for today's garden enthusiasts."

~ **Robert E. Grese,** Director, Matthaei Botanical Gardens and Nichols Arboretum; Professor, University of Michigan School of Natural Resources and Environment

The Spirit *of* Stone

The Spirit of Stone

Stone

of

101 Practical & Creative Stonescaping Ideas for Your Garden

Jan Johnsen

St. Lynn's
press

PITTSBURGH

The Spirit of Stone
101 Practical & Creative Stonescaping Ideas for Your Garden

ISBN-13: 978-1-9433661-9-4

Library of Congress Control Number: 2016958267
CIP information available upon request

First Edition, 2017

St. Lynn's Press . POB 18680 . Pittsburgh, PA 15236
412.381.9933 . www.stlynnspress.com

Book design – Holly Rosborough
Editor – Catherine Dees
Editorial Assistant – Christina Gregory

Photo credits: All photos © Jan Johnsen, with the exception of the following:
page 30 – © Ivo Vermeulen; pages 17 (left), 23, 25, 37, 82 (top right), 86 (bottom left),
131 and 170 – © Laura McKillop; page 38 – © Chris Hansen; pages 52 and 129 – © Jeff Calton;
pages 103 and 104 – © Loretta Reilly

Diagrams/Illustrations appearing on pages 56, 76, 87, 93, 109, 115, 122, 132 and 141 – Laura McKillop

Printed in Canada
on certified FSC recycled paper using soy-based inks

This title and all of St. Lynn's Press books may be purchased for educational,
business or sales promotional use. For information please write:
Special Markets Department . St. Lynn's Press . POB 18680 . Pittsburgh, PA 15236

10 9 8 7 6 5 4 3 2

for Daniel

Table of Contents

A close-up of the stone steps in the Sunken Garden of the Santa Barbara Courthouse in Santa Barbara, California. Note how the top or tread of the step overhangs the riser; this allows rainwater to easily flow off the step and visually highlights the step edge.

Introduction

◞

Unresponsive, rude are the stones;
Yet in them divine things lie concealed…
~ Helen Keller, "The Song of the Stone Wall"

Stone is often an overlooked player in a landscape. While we may swoon over the many shapes and colors of plants within a garden, the stone walks and walls stand silently by, perhaps unnoticed. This book shines a light on the beauty and enchantment that natural stone adds to an outdoor setting. It is a celebration of the versatility of solid, durable rock and showcases the many ways stones and stonework can be featured in the landscape.

If you have ever thought about adding this resilient natural element into your garden, then this idea book is for you. In these pages I offer illustrated design tips and practical techniques for using stone in rock gardens, walks, walls, steps – as artful accents, and much more. You will discover how many possibilities are open to you; rocks can be a still, small voice or a dramatic booming song, depending on how you use them. Bringing natural stone and stonework into your garden can elevate it and anchor it, all at the same time.

I have a soft spot for hard rock. During my four-decade career as a professional landscape designer, I have incorporated stone in a large

A rounded white rock sits as a sharp contrast to the orange-red foliage of a threadleaf Japanese maple tree. This stone accent enhances Nature's autumnal beauty in a simple yet effective way.

variety of outdoor settings. It is, in my opinion, an indispensable part of a garden. My love of stone was fostered by my time living in Kyoto, Japan, as a college student years ago. I interned in a landscape architecture office and on weekends I would visit the historic Japanese gardens. I saw how natural stone and stonework was of central significance in their landscapes. I subsequently studied landscape architecture in Hawaii, where I experienced the fiery beginnings of rock by watching molten lava flowing and cooling into lava rock.

As a young adult, I became a rock climber and my relationship with stone deepened. During ascents on New York's Schwangunk Mountains, I would examine the vertical cliffs up close and see the cracks, fissures and protrusions of the rock as a challenge and an opportunity. I learned to place my fingers inside the crevices in the stone as a climber does, which sometimes meant strong handholds and other times a delicate fingertip grip. I later lived near Barre, Vermont, home of world famous granite quarries, and I would stand in awe as I watched giant granite slabs being hewn from the earth. Ultimately, I settled in Westchester County, New York, where rough fieldstone walls, quartz-laden boulders and classic bluestone walks and patios are found in abundance. From these diverse experiences, I have learned to cherish stone's quiet beauty and its steadying qualities.

Here are a few examples of the many ways you can incorporate natural stone into a landscape. And don't forget pebble mosaics, stacked stones, rock steps, stone circles and beyond!

A stone wall can indeed be a work of art. I love this particular modern style wall located in Croton-on-Hudson, New York. The larger pinkish-hued stones protrude slightly, creating interesting shadows and texture.

In *The Spirit of Stone*, I share my appreciation for this earthy material in the hopes that you too will include it, in some way or other, in your surroundings. Each chapter provides an overview of a different aspect of stone and stonework in the landscape. Many of the photos in this book are of landscapes I have created for others, while some are from noteworthy public and private gardens. I aim to offer you inspiration, but ideas need to be applied in achievable ways, and so I address practical installation issues, describe various stones types, offer ideas for situating stones in gardens and landscapes, and suggest plants that are perfect companions alongside rocks and stonework.

Today, you can find so many wonderful and glorious books about plants and how to use them in gardens of all types. Now, I feel, is a good time for rocks and stonework to join them on center stage. I think the Japanese-American artist and designer Isamu Noguchi summed it up nicely:

> Any gardener will tell you that it is the rocks that make a garden. They call them the 'bones' of the garden. Plants of all sorts, however large the trees, are in a way like weeds: they come and go. But the essential quality of a garden is maintained through the solid disposition of rocks.

The Spirit of Stone celebrates the "solid disposition" of rocks and stone features in the landscape. I hope you enjoy this homage to the "bones" of a garden.

One

The Spirit of Stone

~

...when stone is endowed with personality, one can find it delightful company.
~ Tung Chuin

Stone is the original building block of our world. It rises out of the earth, forming mountains, cliffsides and rocky outcrops. Unlike the sky, which is ever-moving, stone is solid and unwavering. It resounds with the energy of a place, which prompted ancient peoples to see large rock formations as endowed with special powers.

Stone is timeless, condensing the present, past and future within its core. This is what the spirit of stone is all about. Andy Goldsworthy, a British environmental artist who works intimately with natural rock explained it this way: "A lone resting stone is not merely an object in the landscape but a deeply ingrained witness to time…"

Today, many people are rediscovering the spirit of stone; along with appreciating stone for its useful durability and rustic beauty, they enjoy the "grounding" that stone features confer upon their surroundings – and on us. Try holding a small stone in your hand. Concentrate on its solidness and feel the weight. After a minute or two you may feel a little more rooted, your energies more levelled out. This is the spirt of stone at work.

Like water, stone in the landscape is a chameleon material of the best kind, able to elicit from us our most creative efforts and imaginative ideas. Its unique appeal lies in its ability to be many things, from a solitary garden feature to an artful wall or a quiet gravel "sea." Best of all, it is the long-lasting quality of resilient stone that makes it so worthwhile. What you create today will weather through the years, forming an enduring backdrop to fleeting flowers and shrubs. Stone stands the test of time, marking and making a place. Andy Goldsworthy said it well, "A stone changes a place with its presence, with time filling it and flowing aorund it, just as a sea or river rock affects the surrounding water by creating waves, pools and currents."

This chapter, The Spirit of Stone, reviews some ways that natural stones have been used historically outdoors, designating a place. It offers new/old ideas for using this earthy material in a garden and, hopefully, will inspire you to see rocks as a living part of a vibrant landscape.

An artful stacked stone sculpture by Thomas D. Kent, Jr. This is a short lived balanced stone art piece that lasts as long as the wind does not blow.

The nature writer Loren Eiseley eloquently described the elusive secret life of large boulders in his book *The Firmament of Time*: "They seemed inanimate because the tempo of the life in them was slow. They lived ages in one place and moved only when man was not looking."

Stones in Place

Stone, with its strength and permanence, was venerated by early cultures. Dimpled by time, rocks were deeply associated with their locale and told the story of a place in every fissure and crevice. Native Americans saw specific large rocks as the "ancient ones" or the "First People." They would address a large boulder as "Grandfather" or "Aged One," because it evoked an all-knowing presence. Naturally, this reverence led our ancestors to bestow meaning upon certain stones and to use them to summon up memories, assure fertility and to signify special areas.

The word "dolmen" refers to prehistoric stone monuments consisting of two or more upright stones supporting a much larger stone. This ancient dolmen is in the Rock Close of Blarney Castle in County Cork, Ireland. It is a large boulder sitting precariously atop rock supports.

Standing Stones

There is a long-lived tradition in many cultures of using standing stones — upright, vertical stones — to exalt a specific place. These tall sentinels were often seen as helpers, such as in the biblical story of Samuel, who installed an upright stone on the site where a victorious battle occurred. It was more than a commemorative stone; it was what he called an Eben-Ezer (Stone of Help).

The 60 ton "Balanced Rock" sits next to a roadside in North Salem, New York. It is the town's designated historic landmark and is perched surprisingly atop three smaller pointed stones. You can walk around it and marvel at its placement. No one is quite sure how it ended up this way—scientists say it is an 'erratic' left by chance when the glaciers receded after the last Ice Age. Others, the descriptive sign says, believe it is a dolmen, a Celtic memorial stone.

You can find
standing stones left
by earlier civilizations
around the world, and
most particularly in
Ireland, Great Britain
and Brittany in northern
France. In France they
are called menhirs,
and there are 1,200
of them in northwest
France alone. They
are thought to have
been used as territorial
markers or early
astronomical calendars,
but no one is certain.

In Crawick Multiverse the standing stones and the boulders are carefully laid out to represent cosmological themes. Constructed from 2,000 boulders found on the site, the "artland" conveys galactic mounds, comet collisions and much more.

Whatever their purpose, their presence still exerts a commanding call.

Today, modern standing stones have the same exhilarating appeal. Charles Jencks, a well-known contemporary landscape artist and designer, used prominent standing stones in the spectacular "artland" and visitor attraction in Scotland known as the Crawick Multiverse. The large stones he placed and the earthworks he created form an inspiring landmark that links the themes of space, astronomy and cosmology. The stones, our most earthy material, are used to symbolically connect to the outer realms in a dramatic and memorable way. The Crawick Multiverse displays standing

stones for us and future generations to enjoy. You can find more information on their website www.crawickmultiverse.co.uk

You can follow in the steps of this ancient tradition and install a standing stone or stones in your landscape. The spare majesty of tall vertical stones — used as a focal point or entry marker — can be quite memorable. Any kind of long, narrow or pointed stone may become a standing stone. You can use a fissured character stone or a smooth, tapered slab marked with long striations; the choice is yours.

The arrangement of these stones can vary as well. They can be solitary boulders, a procession of evenly

spaced spires or a grouping of upright stones. You may choose to install one stone on a wide expanse of lawn, or you can highlight a noteworthy stone by placing it in a plant bed, flanked by a shapely pine tree. Just make sure your stone is deeply embedded in the earth for maximum stability.

The standing stones shown here can be seen in Innisfree in Millbrook, New York. The photo shows a series of pointed standing stones, half covered by the large leaves of common butterbur *(Petasites hybridus)*. The contrast of the fissured, tapered rocks with large round, green leaves is what makes this scene so alluring.

Narrow natural stones, set upright along a road or in a garden make a unique statement. You can place them in a plant bed or alone. Standing stones can be formed of many types of stone: granite, limestone, bluestone, quartzite and others.

A group of standing stones are set within a grassy plant bed. They are counterbalanced by a low-lying natural stone that appears to jut out of the earth. Design by the author.

Choosing a Standing Stone for Your Garden

The best stones to use as standing stones are long, narrow or thin stones that have clear markings, marked grooves or angular protrusions. I think that the more interesting the stone, the better. I like to use coarse granite, because it is available in my part of the world, and I admire its dense character and grainy texture. Granite, an igneous rock, was formed during the fiery beginnings of our earth and is associated with balance, stability and determination. Healers say it is a guardian stone that offers protection and enhances the ability to be practical. It is said to disperse negativity. This is the "gift of granite."

A Napping Stone...

Pets love to soak up the sun while stretched out on a large rock. Why not place a large flat stone in your garden as a napping place for your pet? It is the opposite of a standing stone and can be nestled in some foliage, hidden away.

Your choice of stones to use should be made both with your mind and with an instinctive "knowing" on your part. In fact, choosing the right stone and placing it upright is more a matter of collaboration with the stone than anything else.

This naturally "white-washed" standing stone is in the garden of Phillis Warden in Bedford Hills, New York. The stone sits in a plant bed with a beautiful Japanese red pine *(Pinus densiflora)* as an evergreen backdrop.

The secret is to learn to listen to the wordless instructions of the rock. Your eye may fall upon a stone and you will know that this is the right one to use. After that, it may tell you more. When I set a standing stone, I will look intently at it and let the rock "tell" me if it is correctly placed, at the right angle, etc. I know it sounds odd, but try listening to the stone, and always know there are no wrong choices.

Using Local Stone

Stone that is native to your area can quietly connect you to a place, since it resonates with its surroundings. By becoming familiar with the native stone, we can know the area better. The granite mountains of New England tell a different story than the schist of Manhattan island or the limestone hills of Indiana. Each has a different pulse and impacts us differently.

Using native stone in a garden rather than synthetic materials elevates the garden. The Japanese architect Kengo Kuma likened using local materials to making sushi: "If the journey of the ingredients is too long, the taste of the sushi is compromised. That is a problem that can't be solved by modern technology, and that program of using local material in season is the secret of good taste..."

A standing stone in the Crawick Multiverse designed by Charles Jencks celebrates both the earth and the sky.

Magnetic Rocks

The perception that rocks are lifeless and inert is wrong. In fact, some rocks are magnetic and resonate to the pull of the sun, moon and earth. This eye-opening concept may explain why certain stones are deemed by some cultures to be beneficial in a garden.

This photo is a striking example of a magnetic stone. Its magnetic attraction is so strong that the paper clips adhere to a hand that sits upon the rock! It contains a great deal of magnetite, which is the same stone that ancient mariners used to create their navigational compasses. It is located in the magnificent estate garden Lotusland, in Montecito, California. You can try it there for yourself.

An Artful Cairn for Your Garden

A stacked cairn of local stone sits on the grounds of Phillis Warden's garden in Bedford Hills, New York.

You might want to consider including a stone cairn in your garden. The grace and beauty of these towers of stone add a special meditative quality to a garden and can vary widely in appearance. It is fun to make a cairn! You can choose to simply place stones in a tapered pile using rounded or flat stones of any size. Or you may choose to fashion them into a more shapely form, such as a rounded or egg-shaped structure. If so, use flat stones, because they stack more easily than round ones. They also lock together better, as long as the joints are staggered. There should be no need to chisel the stone if you take time to hand pick each stone.

The size of your cairn depends on its intended purpose and surroundings, but for safety's sake, don't build a cairn that is taller than you. To begin, dig a hole in the ground about 12" down, compact the earth and lay down filter fabric within the hole. This helps make the foundation more sturdy. Install a 6"-thick layer of angular (not rounded) gravel or crushed stone and compact it thoroughly. You can make it a little thicker if you want, just be sure to install in 2-inch layers and compact it thoroughly. Check that the gravel base is level.

Note: Do not install the cairn in a low spot of the property without providing proper drainage. Use several stones or one large stone for the cairn's base, making sure that they cover the entire base, are level and very stable. The base is the most important part!

Lay a second course of stones on top of the first course. Stagger the stones and joints as if you were laying bricks. The cairn can become gradually narrower from its bottom to its top or can be a straight column. If a stone doesn't lie flat on the stone below it, insert a smaller stone to act as a stabilizing wedge. Place larger capstones at the top. It takes practice and patience – slow and steady is the way.

> *A rock pile ceases to be a rock pile the moment a single man contemplates it, bearing within him the image of a cathedral.*
> ~ Antoine de Saint-Exupery

Advice from a Stone Sphere Maker – Devin Devine

A mesmerizing spherical stone creation by Devin Devine.

Devin Devine is a stone mason and artist residing in Pennsylvania. Among other things, Devine builds spherical cairns for his clients. He never calls them cairns but simply "dry stone spheres." He says, "My preference is to build them dry laid, but sometimes well-hidden glue and/or cement may be included in order to protect from vandalism or to make smaller sculptures movable." Devine also sometimes includes small notepaper with his prayers and poems for humanity written on them. He encloses the paper, along with pieces of quartz, in the center of the spheres as he builds it.

Devine writes that "stacked stone spheres are kind of challenging. The risk of collapse is there, especially at the half-way point. And getting the flow just right is not something that I take very lightly. This type of project does involve a bit of play…but overall it really is not so much whimsical or spontaneous, but rather thoughtful and calculated."

You can read more about his process at his website: www.devineescapes.com.

Stacking Stones — Zen Stones

A far simpler variation on making a cairn is simply stacking a column of smooth stones. The sight of tumbled, water-buffed river or beach stones – sometimes known as Zen stones – balanced atop one another quiets us in a very subtle way. Perhaps this is because rounded rock is a soothing sight.

You can create a stacked stone tower anywhere in the garden. I collect a few small, rounded rocks of varying sizes from a local river and trips to the seashore and bring them home. I wash them off in a bucket of water and leave them sitting atop a low wall, waiting for one of my visitors to stack them. It is a fun activity.

Choose a place to balance your stones where it will not be knocked over. I like to build them at a crossing or entrance to a garden. Select three, five or seven rocks and stack them with the largest at the bottom. Here is the challenge! You must find the balance points of your stones by playing with the shapes and their weight. It takes some deft, light touches, but it is enjoyable to do. It is an especially engaging activity for children in the garden. For added drama, you can also highlight the balanced stone tower at night.

Caution: once you stack some stones, you may be hooked. You may become a full blown stone stacking enthusiast and begin to balance larger ones atop one another in precarious places…it all starts with a few stones.

Stacked stones are a simple way to play with stones. Finding the balance point in each rock makes for a relaxing but focused outdoor activity. The result is a stone-on-stone piece of natural art.

You can collect water-smoothed rocks near the seashore or along river banks. Take a few home and try stacking them with kids or friends.

There is nowhere better than a rocky shoreline to practice your hand at stacking stones. This is what Thomas D. Kent, Jr., does when he visits Grindstone Neck in Winter Harbor, Maine, every summer. Kent creates what he describes as "balanced stone sculptures" using the rocks he collects there. He says he finds solace in wandering the beautiful coastline, which is a change of pace from the hustle and bustle of Philadelphia, where he lives. He selects the stones, balances them and then takes a photo. He admits these are ephemeral and says it is not long before a gust of wind upends them or a seagull mistakes them for a stable perch. He notes, "It is a rare thing when I arrive the following morning to find them all still intact."

Stacked stone sculptures silently adorn the coastline in Winter Harbor, Maine. Sculptures by Thomas D. Kent, Jr.

Chinese Scholars' Stones

If you are seeking to place a stone with meaning in your garden, the history of the Chinese scholars' stone may be of interest to you. These strangely shaped limestone rocks, riddled with holes, furrowed and gashed with indentations, are a highly prized feature in traditional Chinese gardens. Scholars' stones have been worn away by water and time and stand like organic abstract sculptures amidst ponds, bamboo and patterned paving. Their fanciful presence is a silent nod to the Chinese belief that these specific stones have supernatural powers that entice beneficial spirits into a garden. However, the accepted appeal of scholars' stones rests on the notion that these fantastical rocks inspire lofty moods. Indeed, scholars' stones stand tall and connote the vertical thrust of mountains. As Confucius said, "The humane man delights in mountains."

In a Chinese garden, the size of the rock is not as important as its character and positioning. They are recognized for their resemblance to mountains or caves, particularly the magical peaks and dark grottoes believed to be inhabited by immortal beings. These unusual, some might say beautiful, rocks are judged on four important criteria:

- thinness
- perforations
- openness
- wrinkling

The most highly prized of these water-worn stones are called Taihu stones, coming from beneath the waters of Taihu lake. These limestone rocks have been collected since time immemorial

Scholars' stones with their strange shapes are considered to have supernatural powers, according to traditional Chinese belief systems. Here, the gnarled stone contrasts with the refined and intricate paving pattern in the Garden of Flowing Fragrance at The Huntington in San Marino, California. The weathered limestone rocks, from Lake Tai, symbolize the eternal.

The tall waterfall in the traditional Chinese Garden of Flowing Fragrance in The Huntington in San Marino, California. is set against a wooded backdrop of oaks and pines. It is made up of limestone from Lake Tai and can be viewed from the Pavilion for Washing Away Thoughts.

deeper. Kemin Hu, an expert on scholars' stones, explained: "Easterners say that scholars' stones share a telepathic connection with human souls." It is the soulful qualities of these stones that make them a desired feature in a traditional Chinese garden. This was the reason that in the late 12th century, the artist Mi Fei, a stone-lover, had a pavilion built in his garden. It was expressly for the purpose of the contemplation of his stones. He even had a favorite stone that he bowed to and addressed as his "elder brother."

The ancient instructions for setting scholars' stones state that they must appear solidly based — with more of the stone beneath the ground than above. When in groups, the stones should never be symmetrically arranged, and if they are stacked to create an overhanging feature, they should be placed so as to avoid any feeling of instability or artificiality. They may be placed under a stately pine or combined with flowers. If they are large, they can be set up in front of big halls. This is useful stone-setting advice for us today as well.

and are rare. They are white or bluish-black and full of deep hollows and holes. It is said that if one strikes these stones they reply with a faint sound. The most highly regarded rocks emit a bell-like ring when struck.

The primary attraction of scholars' stones, however, is not their looks but something

The personal and spiritual affinity felt for some of these stones was shared by the great Tang Dynasty Chinese poet Bai Juyi (772-846), when he wrote:

Then I turned towards my two rocks asking
If they would stay with me when I am old.
They could not speak yet seemed to say
That they would remain my faithful friends.

Japanese Viewing Stones

Special "viewing stones" are featured in the Japanese Garden in The Huntington in San Marino, California. By silently looking at these water-washed stones, so elegantly displayed, you may experience artistic inspiration or, at least, a relaxing mood.

The popularity of the limestone Chinese scholars' rocks influenced the development of the Japanese art form known as *suiseki* or viewing stones. The Japanese had a deep respect for unusually shaped stones, trees, mountains and ponds, believing them to be inhabited by nature deities, so the idea of artful viewing stones was a natural progression. The stones are found in nature, often coming from rivers, and are prized for their natural shape, texture, color and surface pattern. These character stones are untouched by an artisan's hand and are often displayed on special bases for best effect.

Like other art forms, Japanese viewing stones can be valued for their abstract essence. They may also be prized for their resemblance to perceived realistic scenes and are placed in categories such as Distant Mountain Stone, Stream Stone, Thatched Hut Stone, Human-shaped Stone and more. They may be set outdoors as a weatherproof art piece, and the best part is that visitors are encouraged to touch them!

Today, viewing stones have fans in the United States. In California, for instance, the natural stones run larger than the suiseki in Japan and can be dramatically colored. Many are prized by Japanese collectors. You can find more information from the website www.suiseki.com.

Eroded by water over eons, this black rock looks like a sensuous abstract sculpture. Viewing stones are carefully set on a constructed base, as shown here, and can be placed throughout a garden.

Split Rocks — Intriguing Native Stones

On a walk in the woods, you may find a large boulder or bedrock with a natural split in it. It may appear as if it is cleaved in two parts. These long crevices, extending the length of the boulder, were considered doorways to the underworld by Native Americans. Although too small for a person to physically enter, it was believed that spirits from beneath the surface travelled upward and passed through these narrow openings into the light. To appease the spirits, a single stone or carefully placed smaller stones would often be wedged into the split. In certain wooded parts of the U.S., you can still come across these stones.

The large split rock shares the spotlight with the summer grasses and blooming perennials at the Native Garden at the New York Botanical Garden: native plants such as prairie dropseed (*Sporobulus heterolepsis*), yellow flowering Coreopsis, fall asters.

I saw this boulder sitting along a country driveway as I drove by. I quickly turned back to take this photo. Notice the smaller stones wedged in the cleft – a Native American tradition.

You can see the dramatic large Split Rock at the New York Botanical Garden where it is one of the defining features of the Native Plant Garden. Divided by glacial movement eons ago, Split Rock remains unmovable and static as the luminous meadow grasses dance in the breeze. Its crevice is like a doorway for unseen visitors to emerge amidst the eye-catching foliage and blooming asters. This beautiful garden scene would not be the same without the punctuation of an enigmatic split rock.

Stone Circles

Our ancestors often set specific rocks in a circular arrangement to define special gathering places or to act as astronomical calendars. While some of these constructions are beyond the practical scope for most of us, you can easily make a circle of stones, patterned after the Native American council ring, in your backyard.

A stone circle can be made using upright slabs or large rocks that you can sit on. Whichever shape rocks you choose, try to find stones that contain a high percentage of quartz crystal embedded in them. This is because quartz is a conductor of energy that some of us can feel. It is piezo-electric and resonates in frequency fairly closely to our bones – because our bones respond in the same way a tuning fork hums to certain sounds.

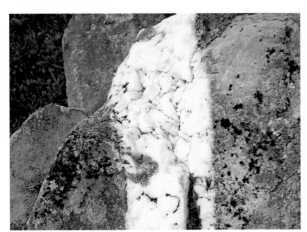

Some stones exhibit stripes of white quartz crystal encased in the body of the rock. Quartz is a conductor of energy that some of us can feel.

The "bluestone" granite of Stonehenge, the most famous stone arrangement in the world, contains a high quantity of quartz and feldspar. Many prehistoric natural stone monuments seem to share the characteristic of containing large amounts of quartz.

Three Tips for Making Your Stone Circle

1. If you create a stone circle, make sure the diameter is the right size. Don't place them so far apart that you have to shout to each other while sitting on the stones. Paint the points on level ground where you plan to set the stones and stand on those points before you put any rocks in place.

2. Consider how many stones you want. Some people have four stones and place one in each of the four cardinal directions. Others use eight for the eight points on the compass such as northwest, southeast, etc. And some prefer odd numbers and will use five stones, spaced evenly.

3. "Settle the stones" into the earth by digging a slight depression and then setting the rock within it. It is like planting a rock. You can plant a carpet of green Scotch moss and Irish moss around them, or you can also tuck different kinds of thyme at the base — their leaves will release a delightful aroma when you brush against them.

The Plimouth Plantation, a living history museum in Plymouth, Massachusetts, has replicated a Native American "gathering circle" made of sitting stones. One is a large stone of white quartz that faces east to greet the first light of day. The explanatory sign next to the circle says, "...feel free to sit on any stone...the rocks offer an ancient story of their own. They point to the four directions which indigenous people understand as elements of Creation carrying meaning and power."

The material of the stones corresponds to the qualities of the four cardinal directions. The sign explains the specific stone layout saying, "a granite stone bears a natural stripe pointing directly south...the west-facing granite, rust-colored with its iron content...another granite stone points a vein of green quartz directly north..."

Quartz was an important part of a Native American stone circle. One reason that Native Americans valued milky or clear quartz crystals is their belief that quartz contained supernatural power that could be used for various purposes. Quartz was considered solid light and was seen as being connected symbolically to the sun. This belief probably came from the practice of forcefully rubbing two quartz pieces together or striking a small stone against

A stripe of quartz crystal makes this stone stand out among others.

a piece of quartz crystal. The friction causes the quartz to emit white light. This is called triboluminescence and is not a spark but essentially pure light. The mechanical action causes the electrons in the atoms to absorb energy. When the electrons return to their usual state, the energy is released in the form of light coming from the interior of the crystal.

* * *

The spirit of stone can be found in the stones we use in our landscapes and those that sit alone on the beaches, in the woodland, in the prairies and rocky cliffs. Their silent song is the one we celebrate in our rock gardens. The next chapter focuses upon rock gardens and explores how we can work with stones to create outstanding landscapes.

Two

In Praise of Rock Gardens

~⌒

As a rule a rock garden should not be near the house; it is something savoring
of the wild that does not fit in with most architecture.

~ Henry S. Adams

In my part of the world, northeast United States, there are rocks and more rocks. If you are a gardener, the urge to combine rocks with plants is a natural one. This endeavor can begin a lifelong love of rock gardens as it did for me. And the one thing that I have discovered is that there are as many styles of rock gardens as there are rocks.

It is all dependent on what you want and where you live. They can be expansive and dramatic or small and quiet. They may be located along a road, by the beach or in an urban backyard. In this chapter, I describe various rock garden styles and focus on the rocks and their placement.

Heat-loving plants such as agave *(Agave americana)* and Mexican feathergrass *(Nassella tenuissima)* thrive in the Gravel Garden in Chanticleer, a Philadelphia-area "pleasure garden." Planted on an open slope, the Gravel Garden features granite steps, stone benches and gravel mulch that surrounds heat-loving, drought tolerant plants.

In rock gardens, the stones are the show. Their character may instill a feeling of a "savoring of the wild," as H. S. Adams noted in his classic book *Making a Rock Garden*. In these gardens, rocks of all sizes and textures are set solidly into a natural setting with few straight lines or symmetry. They need not be complicated and are basically a habitat where plants and rocks co-exist. Here are a few ideas:

- A single existing boulder can be enhanced with a few additional rocks scattered nearby.
- A steep stony bank or outcrop can be planted up with some selected plants.
- A small rocky channel can run through an expanse of carefully placed rocks and succulents.
- A rocky hill can become a showcase for a collection of plants and stones.

Where to Locate a Rock Garden

The recreation of a mountainous rocky landscape was a popular endeavor in the past, when the classical advice was to set a rock garden away from the house and beyond the outdoor living area. But today, current styles have widened beyond the original alpine model and rock gardens can be established wherever you want. You are free to create what you like – where you like – with the understanding that, above all, rocks are the essential component. Even the name has changed; rock gardens are now commonly called rockeries. This moniker embraces all kinds of man-made rock environments.

Rockeries can fit in with the most irregular of sites, such as hot, rocky outcrops or forgotten side yards. It does not matter if there is sun or shade because rocks withstand any environment. The plants, however, must be suited to the light conditions you provide. The stones can be accompanied by sun-loving sedums or by

The rock garden in Bartholdi Park, part of the U.S. Botanic Garden, located in Washington, D.C., is an example of the "hill and crest," where the land slopes up to show off the rock garden denizens.

This colorful rock garden was created by Chris Hansen, plant breeder and hybridizer of SunSparkler® Sedums. The succulents and perennial flowers share the spotlight with the beautifully placed rocks.

a collection of hardy shade-tolerant ferns. A cautionary note: do not create a rock garden beneath a tree with greedy or inhospitable roots or dense shade such as a Norway maple *(Acer platanoides)*. The roots may fight with the plants for water and prevent the rocks from being set deeply into the earth, while the leaves may cast so much shade that few plants can thrive.

Rock gardens can be located to act as a distinct break between other outdoor areas. For example, a garden of stones and plants may break up a long, monotonous walk or become an interesting destination in a hidden corner. You can create a rock garden on an existing slope or, with a little imagination, you can mound up some soil and make a small rise with rocks set within. This follows the "hill and crest" ideal, where rocks of varying sizes are set in a slope behind and above each other. It is a good idea to plant a backdrop of tall plants to show off this scene. You can also weave a rock or mulched path through the garden. That is what I did in the following example, described in the next few pages.

Did you know?

The art of the stone arrangement in Japan is called *sute-ishi*. 'Sute-ji ' means build and 'ishi' means stone. It was considered the main element of a gardener's work.

Sequence for Making a Flowering Rock Garden on a Small Slope

If you have a small slope and a supply of stones, you can convert it into a rock garden featuring low-growing flowering plants. In one overgrown hillside garden, I did just that, rearranging some existing stones and adding larger rocks from the site. You should add several larger stones to act as anchors to give a garden some visual weight and create interest. In this garden, I installed a curving narrow path leading through the rocks and plants. It is for tending to the plants and it also leads the eye through the garden. A small path is a good way to create a unified scene.

The rock garden before we started. Rocks are scattered around without an overall composition. There is no backdrop of taller plants to bring the garden in the foreground in focus.

The rock garden during the transformation. You can see the curving path with small rocks used as steps. Some larger rocks were brought in, smaller rocks were rearranged and we planted small plants around them. No backdrop plantings have been installed.

Here is the sequence we used to renovate this small rock garden:

1. **Stockpile the stones**

   First, we dislodged the rocks from the hillside garden and stockpiled them nearby.

2. **Bring in some large stones**

   We brought in a few larger stones from another part of the property. We used a tree dolly, similar to a hand truck, to move the large rocks. I always try to use rocks from the area, if possible, because they are "at home" here. Also, try to use a single type of native rock, of the same color and makeup, for a cohesive appearance.

   If you buy stones from a quarry or stoneyard, select stones when they are dry and not silt-covered so you can know the real color of the stone.

3. **Dig up and save existing plants**

   We carefully dug up the existing small plants and set them aside. We mulched them and watered them for safekeeping.

4. **Lay out the path**

   I laid out a narrow curving path leading up the rise with "marking" paint (this looks like spray paint but is specifically for marking the ground). Note – you can always redo your markings, so be free when you do this and then step back to review. If you don't like it then erase the paint and try again. We removed a few inches of soil to denote the path and tamped the earth with a tamper.

5. **Cover the area with good soil**

   I applied a thick layer of good soil over the site. If you have a sunny site, use a soil mix that is light and freely draining. I used a mix that had 2/3 topsoil and 1/3 compost. If you are planting plants that like dry conditions, make sure to add very small gravel into the soil for efficient drainage. Rake it smooth.

6. **Place the rocks**

   Now you are ready to "plant" your rocks. I like to use that term because, in a sense, that is what you do in a rock garden. I first added a few flat rocks as steps in the path that went uphill. I then set the larger rocks, in a naturalistic fashion, into the hillside. To do this, you position the rocks the way you like them, then dig them in, backfilling behind the rock with good soil. I often fill behind a rock to set it in a more upright stance, or I may dig it in deeper to make it appear as if it juts out of the earth. See Seven Tips for Placing Rocks in a Rock Garden, on page 45, for advice on setting rocks in the garden.

   In order to set rocks, you must be able to maneuver them around. To do this you should have a crowbar, a large digging bar, shovels,

Here is the rock garden when it was finished. I planted low growing, flowering perennials for eye-catching summertime color. I also used rocks as steps in the path. Many of the plants are spreaders and need to be pruned often to reveal the rocks. It features sedum, campanula, dianthus and perennial geranium and others. In the background is a dark green backdrop of dense yew *(Taxus x media densiformis)* and the yellow Missouri evening primrose *(Oenothera missourensis)*.

strong arms and a strong back. I heartily recommend that you have help for this part of the endeavor! You do not want to put your back out or give yourself a hernia.

7. **Place and plant the plants**

Now comes the fun part – planting up the rock garden. I placed the plants that we had set aside. I spread the plants around the garden, making sure to alter the foliage types and color to create contrast.

Once the plants are in the locations you like, dig the holes and do not plant too deep.

I intentionally placed them close together to minimize weeding. Other people plant more sparingly to enjoy each plant individually. It is your choice. Do not use plants that spread too aggressively because the rocks in this garden should be as much of the show as the plants.

For specific rock garden plant suggestions, see Chapter 8, Plants and Stone.

8. **Mulch, water and admire**

Water in the plants thoroughly. Then cover the surface with a 1" layer of very fine organic mulch and water again. You can also use a thin layer of fine gravel as a covering in a rock garden; this is especially appropriate for a "dry garden" that contains a majority of Mediterranean plants. Water the plants well until established, especially during spells of dry weather.

Rock Placement Tips from Ancient Japan

The 11th century Japanese garden manual *Sakuteiki* says to listen to "the request" of the rocks. They will tell you how best to place them. Shunmyo Masuno, a Japanese Zen Buddhist priest and contemporary garden designer, agrees and says one must "converse" with the stone, waiting "until it seems to speak and say where it wants to be put." So don't feel silly if you think the rock is unhappy in a certain position – move it!

Additionally, the *Sakuteiki* further explains how to set rocks: "Make sure that all the stones, right down to the front of the arrangement, are placed with their best sides showing. If a stone has an ugly-looking top you should place it so as to give prominence to its side. Even if this means it has to lean at a considerable angle, no one will notice. There should always be more horizontal than vertical stones. If there are "running away" stones there must be "chasing" stones. If there are "leaning" stones, there must be "supporting" stones."

Moving Large Rocks

Give me a lever and I can move the world

~ Archimedes

Do not try to move large rocks simply with brute strength! Bending at the waist and heaving up a rock is an invitation to a wrenched back or worse. To maneuver a rock, you can move it, roll it, slide it or flip it over end to end. And, of course, you can use a rock sled, hand truck, ramp or lever.

Move it

A good wheelbarrow is handy, but better still is a two-wheeled hand truck or dolly, because they are lower to the ground and more stable. There are also versatile work carts on the market that come with straps to carry large rocks. These require less lifting power. Use a hand truck with large pneumatic tires to better transport heavy loads, such as large flagstones or rocks, across lawns and uneven or rough ground.

You can use a tree cart, or tree dolly, to move large rocks around. These can be rented at a local rental center.

Roll it

To move large rocks into place, I have used hefty PVC pipes as rollers. This moving technique works best on flat ground and you will need at least one helper to shift the pipes while you roll the rock forward. Use at least three pieces of 4"-diameter

"Schedule 40" PVC pipe. Lift the front of the stone and place two pipes underneath so that the stone rests on the pipes. Set a third pipe in front of the stone so that you can roll the stone forward it. Then when the rear pipe comes free you quickly grab it and place it in front of the rock and repeat.

Lift it

If you need to lift a heavy stone, keep the strain to a minimum. Use a commercial grade product such as the "Potlifter" that is designed for this task. It has lifting loops and lets you insert carrying poles. By grabbing the pole handles, between two to four people can lift rocks weighing up to 350 pounds and up to 34" in diameter.

The product known as a PotLifter™ lets two people grab and twist the handles, as shown, to carry large rocks. Don't forget to wear work gloves!

By inserting carrying poles within the open handles, several people can lift rocks weighing up to 350 pounds. Having the right tool helps in these situations.

Wear Gloves When Working with Stones

If you carry stones or handle any big outdoor job, it is important to wear protective gloves to guard against punctures, cuts and skin abrasion as well as protection against cold and wet conditions. Look for well-fitting gloves that have a wrist closure. This provides an extra-close fit that prevents things from getting inside the glove. Dorian Winslow, president and owner of Womanswork, manufacturer of gardening gloves and much more, says the most important things to look for in a work glove, besides good fit, are good grip and materials that offer good resistance to abrasion. This applies both to leather or non leather gloves with features such as doubly reinforced fingertips and padded palms.

Seven Tips for Placing Rocks in a Rock Garden

You may think that placing rocks in a slope or on a flat plain is no big deal, but in fact, there are several considerations that go into making an appealing rockery. Below are some guidelines; as with most things, they are only suggestions. Feel free to do what makes sense to you.

2. There should be more rocks that sit horizontally than vertically. This "grounds" the scene.

1. Bury the rocks at least 1/3 in the ground to create a natural appearance. You can bury deeper if you want.

3. Have the natural "face" of the rock visible, in accordance with how it was positioned in nature.

4. If the rocks are stratified or have lines, locate the rocks so that these lines run in the same direction with each other. This ensures that they don't look scattered and strewn about.

5. Slant the rocks slightly to direct rainwater into the soil.

6. Locate larger stones toward the base of the slope and smaller ones uphill. This mimics nature in a way.

7. Space the rocks to create crevices where you can tuck in creeping plants that will wander over nearby stones.

The Cactus Garden in Lotusland in Montecito, California, shows how incorporating spiny cacti in a modern rock garden can work.

A Cactus Rock Garden

A very different kind of rock garden can be found in Lotusland, a stunning 37-acre public garden in Montecito, California. The dramatic Cactus Garden makes up three-quarters of an acre and features diorite boulders, a coarse-grained igneous rock, a series of sandstone steps and unusual columnar cacti. This striking rockery was made possible by the donation of an outstanding cactus collection and was arranged by the landscape designer, Eric Nagelmann. He placed vertical columns of basalt stone throughout the garden to highlight the sculptural qualities of the tall plants. He also created deep planting beds among the stones and filled them with specially formulated soil suited for desert plants. The Cactus Garden is a powerful testament to the beauty of elemental stone and exotic cacti.

The Cactus Garden at Lotusland shows us new ways to use natural stone in an arid garden. The sky is the limit when it comes to style and placement, as long as you supply the correct environment preferred by the plants. If you can get some tall narrow stones, why not try a version of this contemporary artful garden in your property?

Exotic cacti such as species of *Opuntia*, endemic to the Galapagos Islands, make their home alongside specially arranged boulders.

The garden is mulched with one hundred tons of shiny black slate chips from a slate mine on the American River near Placerville, California. The dark-colored slate mulch serves to reduce weeds and retain heat in the root zone to keep the cacti happy.

An angular basalt block set as a standing stone reflects the forms of the tall cacti that surround it in Lotusland.

The orange daylilies planted around this rock outcrop are a vivid companion to the bright yellow coreopsis and the blue agapanthus. I planted blue flowers and evergreens to counterbalance the orange. A summer delight for the eye.

A Summer Flowering Rock Outcrop Garden

Large rock outcrops can be outstanding by themselves but, if you are like me, sometimes the urge to add plants within and around a large rock is too strong to resist. In the rock garden shown here, I added topsoil and compost and then planted a wide variety of flowering plants along with ground-hugging sedums and evergreens. The result is a dressed-up rock outcrop that dazzles in the summer. It is not a dry garden – it is irrigated, which allows the flowering plants to flourish.

Because outcrops do not contain much soil, you either have to bring some in or use plants that do well in rocky environments. Some of the best plants for little soil and moisture are the many varieties of creeping sedum, a ground-hugging perennial often known as stonecrop. These durable plants easily make themselves at home in the cracks of a rock. They love sun and good drainage and can spread quickly over a rocky face.

If a rock outcrop seems to be an intrusion into a scene, the best thing to do is to highlight it rather than try to hide it. In one landscape I designed, we unearthed a large outcropping. Rather than remove it, I cleaned off all the embedded soil with a hose and scrub brush. I must admit I love to do this – it is like finding buried treasure.

If there is a theme to this chapter on rock gardens, it is that rocks make great companions to plants, if the plants are chosen well. And don't fret if you have a property with a preponderance of rocks or outcrops – look at this as an asset instead of a problem. You can make spectacular rock gardens there. It depends on your point of view, after all.

Of course, after all the talk about planting up a rock outcrop, you can also just expose the rocks and clean them off as I did in one of my landscape

A large tree coming out of the rock had died so we cut thick slices to make wood pavers lead through the rock garden. The wood turned silvery gray which blended well with the gray Dusty Miller, yellowish sedum, violet *Gomphrena* 'Buddy Purple' and dark purple petunias.

In late August the rock garden is topped with heat tolerant sedum. The red grasses such as 'Fireworks' variegated red fountain grass *(Pennisetum setaceum* 'Rubrum' 'Fireworks')* and violet globe amaranth *(Gomphrena* 'Buddy Purple')* make a wonderful contrast to the dark gray of the stone.

Here is the rock outcrop after we built the curving wall and backfilled with good soil mix. The Flower Carpet® Pink Supreme roses flourish against the rocks.

projects shown here. We removed some of the soil that covered the rocks (with pointed shovels and hand trowels) and then brushed off the remaining soil with a strong scrub brush. Finally, we washed off and cleaned the rocks with a narrow nozzle attached to a hose. It is important to use a hose nozzle with a strong concentrated spray.

We brought in good topsoil (a key factor!) and applied grass seed around the rocks. The grass is trimmed using a weed-whacker, and you must have adequate moisture to keep it looking good. The gray rocks, jutting out of the green turf, make an eye-catching feature in the landscape.

We uncovered this rock outcrop and built a low stone mortared retaining wall in front, as shown above.

A Crevice Garden

Crevice gardens make a fascinating outdoor feature. They can be created on any scale so that even if you have limited space, you can enjoy this unique kind of rock garden. Instead of placing rounded rocks into mounded soil, you push flat slabs of stones, such as flagstone or slate, into the soil vertically from the top. Space these thin pieces close together and fill the narrow channels with lean, gritty and well-drained soil. A good mix is 1/2 soil and 1/2 small crushed stone, and a fertilizer especially formulated for dry gardens. Use a chopstick or skewer to force soil into the crevices.

Plant small rock garden plants that fit within the crevices. Many of these plants have deep-growing tap roots that need fast-draining soil. Their roots will grow down to a depth where temperature and moisture are more stable, promoting faster and heathier growth.

The vertical rock spacers help to channel rain down into the soil, which waters the plants but keeps the soil dry on top. Make sure there is good drainage at the base so the water flows through the soil quickly. Planting bare root plants in dry soil is best. Water thoroughly twice after you plant. Mulch with 1/2" of fine crushed gravel.

Rockery plants are widely available. Many may be found in a separate section labelled as "Alpines" and are relatively cheap to purchase. Other plants that are suitable for the rockery, such as dwarf conifers, will be stocked in separate areas.

You can also create a crevice garden in a trough. Find some thin stone slabs and place them in a suitable container, as Jeff Calton did here. His slab garden is about 4' long by 2' wide and about 2' high at the highest point. He used crushed granite in the bottom of the crevices then filled them with a gritty succulent soil mix of half soil mix with half 1/8" pumice. The positioning of the vertical stones is as interesting as the small plants that are growing in the crevices.

The Gravel Garden

Gravel gardens are an example of a rock garden that is perfect for sunny, hot areas where drought-tolerant, Mediterranean-type plants thrive. In recent years, gravel gardens have become popular, especially in drought-stricken areas. But they can be created anywhere as long as the site is very well drained. This is because a gravel garden is, above all, a dry garden. Beth Chatto, the highly respected English gardener and author, described it best when she wrote about growing drought-tolerant plants: "It's like gardening on the beach."

You can choose from a wide variety of colors, shapes, and sizes of gravel to use – from crushed red limestone to granite chips to rounded river rock and more. The stone adds an elemental feeling to a scene. Just the ticket for today's landscapes!

Granite block steps placed in the Gravel Garden at Chanticleer made the garden come alive. The rows of light colored stone form an ordered setting to show off various heat-loving plants.

A Gravel Garden around a Rock Outcrop

If you have a rock outcrop that juts out from a lawn, you might consider creating a gravel garden around it. This is what horticulturist Ed Impara did at Michael Bakwin's property in Ossining, New York. He inserted a few additional flat stones around an existing rock outcrop, installed a diverse assortment of plants, and surrounded it all with small, light–colored gravel that accents the natural gray stones beautifully. The challenge was to find plants that could tolerate rocky conditions and fit the Japanese–inspired style he wanted. Impara planted a golden threadleaf Chamaecyparis and dwarf threadleaf Japanese maple here, which co-exist with ground-hugging sedum and small grass-like sedges.

Within the flat expanse of gravel, Ed placed a piece of aged driftwood. This contorted wood feature, with its deep gray color, rough texture and irregular form is as striking as any art piece. The juxtaposition of the grassy foliage and small gravel makes it especially appealing. Art is most certainly in the eye of the beholder.

A gravel garden works well around rocky outcrops that jut out from a lawn. You should add some good soil around the rock outcrop to make sure shrubs like those shown here can get a good footing in the earth. Top with a mulch of small gravel, as shown.

The Dry Landscape – Karensansui

In Japan, gardens of painstakingly groomed gravel surrounding specially selected rocks are referred to as *karesansui*, or "dry landscape" gardens. This ancient style was developed by Zen Buddhist monks who aspired to embrace the Japanese principle of *yohaku-no-bi,* literally "the beauty of blank space." These rock gardens, sometimes known as Zen gardens, are silent, peaceful places that are not to be walked upon but, rather, to be observed. Their aim is to quiet your thoughts. Originally part of Zen monasteries, they are normally framed by a surrounding wall or fence, which helps to create a quiet retreat from a busy world. Today, these traditional gardens of stone are revered for their simple beauty as well as their historic significance.

The raked gravel dry garden is designed for contemplation. The backdrop of a sheltering wall creates a sanctuary. The gravel is raked to evoke the feeling of moving water. Rocks embedded in the gravel appear as islands in a sea.

Dry landscape rock gardens, although arid, are all about water. Plants are not important – and sometimes nonexistent – in these gravel gardens. Light-colored decomposed granite, small pebbles, or fine gravel is precisely raked into curves and circles, mimicking ripples in a gravel sea. The large stones set within this "sea" connote mountainous islands. If you are interested in creating a Zen garden, choose a site that is relatively level, far from noise or distraction. It does not have to be large; a good size could be a 9' x 15' rectangle or anything you choose. Carefully consider where it is to be viewed from. Historically, dry gardens were designed to be looked down upon from a designated distance, often from a nearby covered balcony, terrace or deck.

After you have chosen the perfect site, remove all vegetation (roots and all) and smooth the area to almost level. Don't forget, you need a slight pitch for rainwater to drain off. Dig out the space to a depth of 3" and tamp to compact the soil. Although gravel and crushed granite help to deter weeds, you may choose to lay filter fabric for greater weed control. Place the island rocks following some of the tips I offer in this book, making sure they are set solidly in the earth.

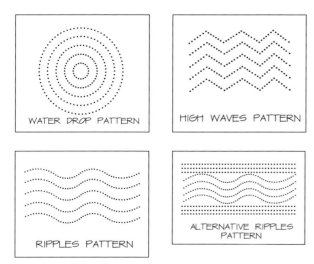

WATER DROP PATTERN

HIGH WAVES PATTERN

RIPPLES PATTERN

ALTERNATIVE RIPPLES PATTERN

Raked ripples and waves are part of a Japanese gravel garden. Start with a leveled out surface, free of debris and leaves, and press evenly using a wood rake with special teeth to create the pattern. Solid-colored light gravel shows off the shadows and light of the pattern more evenly than multi-hued gravel.

Take your time to do this; they should appear natural and random, not symmetrical. My advice is to place the rocks, step back and look at them, and then wait a day before you dig them in.

Now pick a type of crushed stone that packs well and is able to hold raked grooves. Important! Regular beach sand won't retain the curved lines that give dry gardens their distinctive look. Most often a light-colored crushed stone is used. Landscaping suppliers can help calculate the correct amount of rock you need. Please note: if you have a very sunny area, choose a darker stone, as the light gravel will be too glaring. I learned this the hard way when I created a dry landscape gravel garden in a sunny suburban backyard. We had to blend in a darker stone after the sun glare proved to be too much. It was the opposite of a tranquil space.

Also, make sure that the gravel you choose is readily available so that you can replenish or freshen up an area with additional gravel easily. There is nothing worse than finding out that the gravel you used in your garden is no longer available.

Install the crushed stone to a depth of 2" or slightly more and spread it evenly with a hoe. Once the gravel is installed you will have to rake it on a consistent basis. Raking a dry garden improves concentration and is a skilled art form in itself. Japanese gardeners carefully rake a set of lines or ripples drawn across the gravel in swirling patterns, circling each rock to appear like waves breaking around an island. One of the tools for doing this is a specially designed traditional wood rake and the other is a modern lightweight aluminum rake often used on golf courses. The aluminum rake smoothes the gravel and the wood rake creates the grooves and the desired spacing of the gravel ridges. You can lightly wet down the gravel before you rake. Make sure to rake the lines that encircle rocks often because these have the strongest impact and are noticed the most.

I buried this rock halfway into the ground to make it look like a natural outcrop. The light green lichen growing on the rock adds to its interest. It punctuates the field of smooth pink concrete that sites nearby.

Design Tip

The interplay of light is a subtle design feature in a dry landscape garden. The contrast of sun and shadow is an important consideration when positioning and spacing the stones. When the low morning or evening sun casts long shadows in the garden, the texture of rocks and gravel takes center stage. Additionally, light and dark stones are placed together to create a harmonious balance that is on display both during the day and especially on a full moon night.

* * *

Once you see how beautiful stone can be in a rock garden, it is a natural step to appreciate its use in other outdoor applications. The next chapter, Sustainable Stone, discusses how stone, in its many forms, can be used in functional ways to make our landscapes more eco-friendly.

Three

Sustainable Stone

~⁀

River stones remain, while water flows away.
~ Romanian proverb

Historically, garden design has focused on creating beautiful outdoor spaces that please us in some way. We are now enlarging that definition to include making landscapes that are sustainable as well as attractive. This means partnering with Nature to minimize adverse impacts on human health and the environment, such as staying away from herbicides and using non-chemical fertilizers. Such a wise move! Paul Hawken, visionary businessman, noted, "the first rule of sustainability is to align with natural forces, or at least not try to defy them." This chapter takes a look at some of the interesting ways stone can be used in eco-friendly landscapes.

The contrast of the fine grass blades of Mondo grass (Ophiopogon japonicus) against the stone displays a unique Japanese aesthetic. As writer Lafcadio Hearn described in his classic book, *Glimpses of Unfamiliar Japan,* "everything Japanese is delicate, exquisite, admirable."

Natural stone comes directly from the earth and is the original sustainable material. It is 100% recyclable, can be cleaned with water, does not emit any harmful vapors, and endures for lifetimes. It is not created in a factory.

Stone and gravel of various sizes are key to being "green," because they can be used as drainage, mulch, and for erosion control. Rocks can help stormwater drain into the earth instead of being channeled into pipes that outlet into our waterways. This sustainable use of stone alleviates seasonal flooding, naturally filters polluted drain water and prevents heated water (from roofs and hot roadways) from afflicting fish and amphibians.

Rediscovering an Ancient Drainage Technique

Traditional Japanese artisans used stone in inventive yet functional ways. The climate in Japan is fairly rainy, so it was a common practice to raise a Japanese house a foot or two off the ground. Around and beneath these classic structures, the earth was carefully covered with gravel or small stones. This is elegantly demonstrated in the Japanese Garden in The Huntington, in San Marino, California. Here, an original Japanese house dating from the early 20th century sits on sturdy posts set on small granite bases surrounded by a generous area of gravel.

The gravel is attractively edged with a line of medium-sized rounded rocks buried halfway in the earth. Outside of this is a one-foot-wide channel of dark gray river stones held in place by a weatherproof board. The contrast of the size, shape and color of the various stones is both beautiful and distinctive.

The function of the gravel field is to allow excess rainwater to percolate into the ground, preventing any wetness beneath the house. This use of stones can be adapted to any style of house and landscape.

Another Japanese sustainable technique is their decorative drainage channel. This attractive stone feature can embellish a patio or walk and also collect rainwater runoff. It edges a patio on one side and is held in place by curved clay or fiber cement roof tiles on the other. You can see an example of this at the Portland Japanese Garden, in Portland, Oregon.

Instead of curved roof tiles, you can use one-foot-wide stone pavers, 1" thick, set vertically on their side as a border. The important thing to do is to install at least a 6–8"-deep layer of gravel beneath the upper layer of rounded stones to facilitate drainage. A pipe can also be inserted into the gravel, 2/3 of the way down into the channel, to carry the water away. Remember to pitch the pipe slightly in the direction you want the water to run.

This drainage channel is filled with small, gray, rounded stones. The differences in the color and size make it a visually compelling scene. When you go to the landscape supply store, choose carefully from the wide variety of stones in order to ensure contrast.

Gravel: A Popular, Sustainable Choice

Here is a display of gravel types at a supply yard. Often they will give you a small plastic bag of sample gravel to take home.

Gravel is a versatile and essential item in the sustainable landscape toolkit – weatherproof, easy to install and requires no mowing, watering or fertilizing. It is relatively cost effective and easy to transport. And it works well in all climates. In arid regions, gardeners use it in place of lawns or as heat-reflecting mulch around plants. In wetter climates, they like that gravel is quick draining, a necessary quality for walks and drives. No wonder it is such a popular material and used in so many outdoor applications!

The term "gravel" refers to either small rounded pebbles or crushed stone. It is increasingly available in a wide variety of colors, shapes and sizes. Some areas get their gravel from local rivers and have large supplies of natural gravel. However, in areas where river-run gravel is hard to come by, gravel is produced by mechanically crushing hard rocks into several sizes. This is called crushed rock. Natural gravel tends to be rounder, smaller and lighter in weight than many types of crushed stone.

Garden designers like using gravel because it is so malleable and the design possibilities are numerous. It fits in with French, English, Colonial, Japanese and modern American style gardens. The small stones add an elegance and sophistication when contained in crisp, straight walks in a contemporary landscape. And gravel's range of colors can be used to create a vivid contrast with other garden elements when used as stone mulch in sprawling, free-form plant beds. And of course, traditional gray gravel creates a classic country driveway.

One sustainable design idea is to insert a border of gravel at least 18" wide or more between a paved walk and open lawn. It serves as a visual break and can catch water that runs off the sidewalk without puddling in the lawn or plant bed. The line can be a gently wavy line of gray gravel or even red lava rock that contrasts with the sidewalk. Add a few bold succulent plants as sculptural accents in a small plant bed if you like.

Also, you can create a level gravel field in which to "float" things like larger stones or individual plants. Just remember to use darker gravel that doesn't create glare – I learned that the hard way.

What is Stone Dust?

Stone dust is stone screenings that have been crushed into a powder. When it is packed down it forms a hard surface that does not drain and is water resistant. This ability to form a non-porous surface makes it a good joint filler between pavers in patios and walkways, because it prevents water from seeping down into the base and keeps weeds and grass from growing.

What is Crushed Stone?

Crushed stone is rock that has been quarried and mechanically crushed. It can range in size from 1/4"–1-1/2" and is produced from many types of stone such as granite-gneiss, trap rock, limestone, quartzite or any combination of these materials. It is sold in different sizes and colors, each suitable for different uses. For example, 1-1/2" crushed stone is used for gravel driveways and to enhance drainage, while the larger 2-1/2-" crushed stone is used as stone mulch to prevent erosion on roadsides.

Crushed stone has naturally jagged edges and angled planes, which make it easier to interlock together. This means it packs well to make a stable walking or driving surface or foundation. Always get a sample to check the size of the stone on site before you order a large load to be delivered!

A Few Types of Gravel

The availability of different types of gravel depends on where you live. Your nearby stone yard will carry locally sourced "native" gravel and some imported stone that is trucked in from far away locales. The availability of gravel types – and their names – varies greatly with your location. For this reason, it is best to check with your local stone supplier about which gravel type will best suit your needs and how much you require.

Large gravel, 1" or more, is best used for drainage and backfill, while 3/4" gravel and 3/8" gravel is used in drainage, driveways, landscaping and paths. The smallest size, 1/4" gravel, is good for walks and other surfaces. Here are a just a few examples of popular types of gravel:

1. **Pea Gravel**

   Pea gravel is a generic name for small, attractive multi-colored earth-tone pebbles that have a smooth texture, the result of natural weathering. Pea gravel  is rounded and comes in sizes from 1/8–3/8". It gets its name because the stone is similar in shape and size to a pea. It can be used as a surface for paths and patios, but please note that the rounded stones do not compact well. This means they will roll around under your feet or car. For this reason, it is not recommended as a driveway surface. In addition, the smooth small stones can get caught in the grooves of tire treads and may form ruts. Pea gravel is best used as decorative ground cover and for drainage purposes. Its appearance and type differs from region to region.

2. **Decomposed Granite**

   Granite is a hard, igneous rock that naturally comes in various shades of gray, black, brown, pink and tan. Decomposed granite, known as DG, is like crushed gravel, composed of fine 1/4" and smaller particles (fines), some no bigger than a grain of sand. The small DG fines pack well, stay in place and can be raked into a smooth, flat base for walks and patios. It is ideally suited for stable surfaces, once compacted, and works great for low traffic walkways, driveways, garden trails or xeriscape ground cover.

   Crushed granite differs from DG because it has no sand or silt particles, and its particles are larger than DGs. The texture makes it a good choice for contemporary houses and it is a great groundcover for xeric or dry plants. It is not as readily available as DG and it can be more costly. Source: Bourget Brothers, Santa Monica, Calif. (bourgetbros.com)

3. **White Marble Chips**

   This is a bright-white, high-end stone ground cover that reflects heat and light. It can be used around the base of plants, especially heat-loving plants such as succulents and cacti. These irregular, jagged stone chips can be streaked with gray and black and come in sizes 2" or smaller.

4. **Delaware River Rock**

   This is a highly attractive, smooth-textured stone that has been weathered by the water currents of the Delaware River. It is available from pea gravel sizes up to stones 5" or more. It comes in yellow, gold, beige and brown tones with white highlights. An excellent choice to define borders, cover areas where grass is not practical, function as a stone mulch and be used in dry streams and channels.

5. **Red Crushed Stone**
   Burgundy red, decorative crushed stone creates a rustic country landscape that many love. It comes in a variety of sizes from

   3/4–1-1/2". Great for walkways, landscape beds and general landscape applications.

6. **Maryland Shore Bantam Egg Gravel**
   Decorative, rounded stone. The color is in a white and light gray range. Comes in several sizes.

7. **Del Rio Gravel**
   A washed river pebble that ranges in color from speckled gray and white to tan, harvested in Ventura County, California. Perfect for stone

   mulch and water gardens. These pebbles look beautiful underwater. Source: Bourget Brothers, Santa Monica, Calif. (bourgetbros.com)

8. **Red Lava Rock**
   This gravel is a colorful, crushed rock created by volcanic activity. The red color comes from the oxidation of iron. It is a favorite

   for desert landscapes and is a standout in plant beds. Relative to other rock mulches, lava rock is lightweight, so it is less costly to transport and less difficult to spread as a mulch. It may blow away in windy areas, and its sharp edges can damage mower blades if pieces blow onto lawns.

9. **Jersey Gold 3/8"**
   The small stones are rounded and feature yellow, tan, beige and brown stones. Jersey Gold is used for garden paths, driveways, drainage and mulch. Great

   under trees and between stepping stones. Makes a nice contrast with grey stone curbs and edging.

A wide, fine gravel walk in the Berkshire Botanical Garden in Stockbridge, Massachusetts, is edged by thin metal edging to create a defined line. It is important to hold in the stone material and form a separation between the plants and walk. The large yellow shrub is Tiger Eyes sumac *(Rhus typhina* 'Tigereye Bailtiger'*)*.

Gravel Walks

Gravel walks invite us into a garden. They are not as formal as a paved walk but are durable and long lasting. Gravel is a good choice for a walk if you want a soft mood and a neutral color that fits in with plants and flowers. They reflect less heat than a paved walk and don't puddle as long as they are slightly pitched. You should crown a path so that the center is slightly higher by an inch or two than the sides to ensure that water will run off or percolate down. *Caution:* don't slope a gravel path excessively, because the loose gravel will move or be washed away.

There are a few other cautions with gravel walks. Do not have a gravel walk come up directly to your door, because the small gravel pebbles may stick to your shoes and end up marking up your floors.

This secondary path, made from larger gravel, is in the garden of Michael Bakwin in Ossining, New York. It allows drainage and is an easy way to access the extensive plantings in wide beds. You can see this inspiring landscape during the Open Days sponsored by the Garden Conservancy.

Make sure there is a hard paved landing area by the door to act as a "door mat" where the gravel can fall off the soles of the shoes. Gravel walks are also tricky to shovel in a snowy winter, and the pebbles can end up in the lawn and plant beds when you clear the snow. Lastly, it hurts to walk on gravel without shoes!

The best gravel to use for a walk is angular stone, 3/8" or 1/4" size. The jagged, irregular pieces pack well together to provide a stable surface for walking. This is a good choice for well-used walks, as the stones bind together and do not scatter. Decomposed granite also provides a firm surface to walk on. You may like the look of the smoother pea gravel better, but remember that the stones, being round, can move more easily, making it

more difficult to walk on. This is especially true for driveways, where it is best to use angular gravel.

A gravel walk or path should be installed on a sturdy subbase of coarser, well-compacted crushed stone or item #4 base (also called quarry process). Excavate to a depth of 7" (or more, depending on your climate) and pitch very slightly in one direction for drainage. It is important to compact the earth base with a roller or tamper. Lay a 2–3" base layer of crushed stone within the excavated area and thoroughly compact the stone subbase. Now lay down another 2" layer of crushed stone and tamp thoroughly again. The compaction is very important! Lay geotextile filter fabric on top of the subbase, then install a 2"-thick layer of decorative crushed stone or small gravel atop this. The filter fabric prevents the smaller stones from percolating down into the stone subbase. Some people advocate laying the crushed gravel directly on bare, compacted earth; if you do, just make sure the earthen base is weed free and is pitched to drain water away.

What is "Item #4"?

Item #4 is known by various names, including Quarry Process (QP). It is a dense grade aggregate, run through the crusher, a DOT-specified material that is made up of a blend of crushed stone and stone dust. It compacts well, is durable and creates a good foundation for road bases, gravel driveways or stone walkways.

A Strong Base for Porous Gravel Paving

Gravel walks are porous and allow water to flow through into the earth. But they can form ruts and may settle, creating an uneven surface. This makes it hard for people in wheelchairs, on bicycles or with strollers. There are several eco-friendly options available if you want a gravel path to be sturdier. You can install specially designed plastic panels with open

Green Driveway® panels set on a path (top) are then filled with gravel. The permeability of this system allows water to seep into the earth, improves storm water management and reduces heat island effect.

cells on a prepared surface on the ground and then fill them with gravel. These panels hold gravel in place and provide a strong base for all kinds of pedestrian uses. Some products can be used for vehicular driveways.

One product, Green Driveway®, offers a variety of gravel and soil stabilizing grid systems. The grids consist of polypropylene panels of hexagonal cells in a honeycomb-like pattern with a geotextile filter attached underneath. The system prevents weed growth and provides structural support without sacrificing drainage. Easy to install – add gravel into the cells and you have an eco-friendly surface that, when filled, is practically invisible. Certain models of this product can withstand over 300 tons of pressure.

The Sound of Gravel

People like gravel's earthy texture and the crunchy sound it makes when they walk on it. These two aspects encourage us to slow our pace and enrich our experience of an outdoor space. In old Japan, the "clip clop" footfall sound created by the traditional wooden sandals on a path was a key garden design consideration. Certain stones intensified the sound, so ancient Japanese gardeners alternated solid stone paths with gravel paths to vary the sound of footsteps in the garden. You can do the same thing in your garden.

Stone Edging – a Useful Consideration for Gravel Walks

Gravel walks and paths must be contained with some kind of edging. There are several kinds to choose from – steel, brick, concrete, wood or thin plastic strips – but stone edging is one of the best choices since it is sturdy, requires little maintenance and is long lasting. The following are three stone edging ideas you can use.

A bluestone paver, set on edge, creates a thin gray line separating rounded gray gravel and "stone dust" on the right. A tawny pink concrete paver adds some color.

Bluestone Edging

I like to use thin bluestone pavers set on edge as a border around gravel. The line of the pavers creates a clean, gray frame of stone, as shown here. The top of the edging is flush with the earth and extends at least 12" into the ground for stability. The edging consists of 3' long x 1" thick x 12" wide bluestone pavers set into a concrete base. Concrete ensures that it stays in place, but it is not necessary if the border is set deep enough.

A frame of smooth-edged bluestone makes rounded stones look neater and contained. Note how wet stones look different from dry ones in this photo.

The treatment of the cut edge of the bluestone can be a smooth saw cut or a "thermal" finish, which has a subtle pebbled texture. In the photo at left, the smooth edge contrasts smartly with the river pebbles and fine stone gravel. The juxtaposition of shapes, colors and textures makes this an outstanding scene through all seasons of the year.

Belgian block comes in a variety of colors as shown here. Choose one color for edging or for fun, why not mix them?

Belgian Block or Cobblestone Edging

You can hold in a gravel walk with Belgian block or cobblestone. Belgian block and cobblestone are often confused with each other, but there are differences. Cobblestones are antiques of a sort, having been used for paving for more than 500 years in Europe. The stones were taken from rivers and streams and then hand trimmed and shaped into rectangles and squares. They were set, or "cobbled," into patterns in ancient street paving and became smoothed. Cobblestones are historic, aged and beautiful and can vary in size. Belgian blocks may have gotten their name from the stones originally brought over to America as ballast in ships sailing from Belgium. They are cut in modern quarries as cubical blocks of durable stone (typically granite). They come in an assortment of sizes and colors including black, gray, pink and yellow.

This solid stone is used as curbs but also makes a great edging for gravel walks. To install edging, dig a shallow trench, line it with geotextile filter fabric, then fill it with an inch of crushed stone. Rake the gravel, tamp it and set the Belgian block atop the gravel base layer, making sure they form an even line. When you have the stones lined up perfectly, tamp the soil behind them (you can use a concrete mix if you prefer) and fill the path with gravel. For stability, bury the Belgian block to approximately three-quarters of their depth.

Natural Stone Edging

Almost any stone can be used to border a gravel walk or path. You can go out in the woods and collect rounded stones from the woods or fairly thin ones from a creek bed. They should be easy to carry and maneuver in place, about 9–14" long. You can find those of different colors or choose only stones that match each other. And for those who want to buy them, many home-improvement stores and stone supply yards sell natural stone.

Dig a narrow trench, place a small amount of gravel and then place the stones inside – make sure that at least half the stone should be buried below grade. This is important so that the stones don't move. If possible, fit the stones tightly together for a uniform appearance and then hit them with a rubber mallet to make sure they are set firmly in the earth.

Rounded stones were set in the earth and used as rustic edging for a gravel walk in Edith Wharton's historic estate, called The Mount, in Lenox, Massachusetts. It is open to the public and you can see this edging, covered with moss, in the lovely sunken Italian Garden. This garden is bounded by tall stone walls complete with porticos and sitting alcoves. A stone lover's delight!

The Native Plant Garden at the New York Botanical Garden features winding, hard gravel paths that travel through woodland, meadow and waterside environments. These wide paths were created using Gravel-Lok™ polyurethane binder, which lets rainwater pass through while retaining the beautiful, natural look of gray gravel. It creates a long-lasting, hard yet permeable surface that maintains the look of a natural gravel walk. There are several similar liquid binder products you can use to create this permeable yet hard surface.

Dry Streams – a Beautiful Way to Catch Runoff

A dry stream is a unique, sustainable way to incorporate natural rocks in a garden and address poor drainage issues. Made to look like a babbling brook, it does not normally contain water, but instead channels and collects rainwater, allowing it to percolate into the ground slowly. It is essentially a shallow depression in the earth designed to slow and capture runoff. I first saw dry streams in Japan decades ago and fell in love with them. They follow the model of a watercourse, filled with gravel and stones and may have plants along the banks.

Dry streams are a great solution wherever there is a need for on-site rainwater drainage. They can be placed at the base of a slope, in a low spot that puddles occasionally or up a small rise to intercept rainwater as it flows downhill. Since dry streams are a small-scale version of a real life landscape feature, they look wonderful in naturalistic gardens. Yet, they also fit in with a variety of landscapes, rural or urban, dry or wet.

I have created several dry streams. Each one is slightly different depending on the area, the rocks used and the site conditions. But the common element in all of them is that they are filled with an 8–12" base layer of coarse gravel, wrapped in filter fabric. The gravel absorbs excess rainwater. Atop the gravel, I place a thin layer of decorative rounded river stone to create a more finished look.

A dry stream edged with rocks collects rainwater naturally and lets it seep into the earth. The red Japanese maple draws the eye down the length of the dry stream.

73

How to Create a Dry Stream

It is not too difficult to create a dry stream. You must have a sufficient number of fairly large-size rocks (about 12–18" long), a roll of filter fabric and gravel to fill in the stream. First, lay out a slightly curving trench and widen it at certain sections. The shape and alignment of a dry stream is important in making it look natural. Think of how water moves through a landscape; streams in nature are not straight channels, they meander back and forth. So make your stream a curving line and be sure to include a wider section where the invisible water "pools." This pool provides a place where you can set larger rocks and maybe an eye-catching plant.

The width of the trench should vary. You can make part of it as narrow as 16" wide (before placing rocks) and other sections as wide as you want. Excavate the trench at least 10–14" deep (or more, if it is meant to act as a deep catch basin). Place the soil from the excavated area on the sides of the stream. I place more soil on the far side of the stream to create a higher plant bed there. This creates interest and works especially well with plants that drape over rocks because they will not grow into the stream bed.

Line the entire trench with filter fabric (not plastic!) and extend it beyond the sides. Set large-size rocks along the stream bank atop the filter fabric. The rocks will be partially covered by the gravel and stone, so no need to worry about how their bases look. You can have the stones protrude higher than the outside ground level or plant bed. It depends on the look you want to create. Jutting rocks have a rugged appearance and create a dynamic look, especially in modern settings. Feel free to experiment with the border stones as you place them. There is no incorrect way of doing it! After they are placed, backfill behind the rocks with good quality soil. The soil may be brought up close to the top of the rocks that border the dry stream, if you want. The soil should not be too clayey and be able to sustain healthy plants or lawn.

Fill the trench with 1/4–1/2" gravel or similar. In very wet situations, add a few inches of gravel, install a 4"-diameter subsurface pipe atop this layer of gravel and connect to an underground catch basin. Then fill the trench almost to the top of the stream. Atop the gravel, carefully install a single layer of rounded pebbles of your choice. The stones contrast beautifully with the rocks on both sides of the stream. You can also use rocks of various sizes as a topper as well.

Planting along the sides of your dry stream is the fun part. In Chapter 8, Plants and Stone, I suggest selected plants you may use.

While building a dry stream, fill the channel with inexpensive gravel. Backfill behind the rocks that border the stream with good soil to ensure that plants flourish. Lastly, top the stream with a thin layer of more expensive rounded rocks as shown at right.

After you dig the channel about one foot deep, lay some filter fabric inside and place rocks along the sides. The rocks on the far side are higher than the ones next to the proposed lawn.

Begin building a dry stream by determining the layout and width of the channel. Remember that rocks along the side will take up some of the width. Make sure to allow for wider "pool" areas. I use orange marking paint (not spray paint!) to denote where to dig.

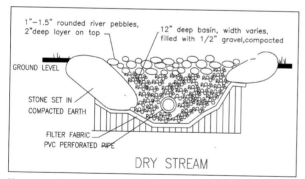

1"–1.5" rounded river pebbles, 2"deep layer on top

12" deep basin, width varies, filled with 1/2" gravel,compacted

GROUND LEVEL

STONE SET IN COMPACTED EARTH

FILTER FABRIC

PVC PERFORATED PIPE

DRY STREAM

You can place a PVC perforated pipe (holes facing down) within the swale, if it is meant to channel water away. Use rocks that look like the native stone in your area. Stay away from blasted rocks as they are too angular.

The finished dry stream. The channel is narrow but stands out with the dark gray Mexican beach pebbles contrasting against the lighter stones. Thin blades of iris and sedges, fitting plants for a streamside planting, enhance the look.

Stone Mulch – Yes and No

The practice of using stones as a groundcover has been growing in popularity, especially in drought-stricken areas where it is used as a replacement for lawn. Stone mulch, as it is often called, consists of a layer of gravel or small rocks installed on top of a plant bed or around a tree. It is admired for its decorative and heat-reflecting qualities and can be used in contemporary settings as well as in urban, rustic and seaside landscapes.

The chief advantage of stone mulch is its long-lasting properties. Unlike organic mulches such as leaves and shredded bark, stone mulch does not decompose or decay, eliminating the need to reapply every year. But stone mulch does not add nutrients to the soil in the same way that leaves and bark can. For this reason, some gardeners stay away from it. In arid regions, however, it is a smart, sustainable way to cover the soil and moderate its temperature. In high wind areas, crushed stone works well where lighter, organic mulches might blow away. It all depends on your intent and location.

Stone mulch can be a great looking material in certain landscapes. Medium-size stones covering the ground in an evergreen garden can add the perfect blend of rugged naturalness with sustainable benefits. It blends well in rocky environments. These kind of stones can be hard to

This rough stone emulates a rocky mountain slope covered with "scree" which is a mass of rocky debris found at the base of crags and mountain cliffs. Scree accumulates over the years from periodic rock fall. It is nature's stone mulch.

walk on, so you can use them to prevent pets and people from entering certain fragile planting areas.

Properly installed, stone mulch can act as a weed barrier. But there are certain things to keep in mind before you install it:

- Avoid placing stone mulch on sloped areas where stones can roll down.
- Do not install it where the small rocks can get run over by a lawn mower, causing damage to the machine.
- Make sure to install stone mulch at least 1" below sidewalk level to reduce its movement out of plant beds.
- Consider the color of the stones, making sure it does not clash with the plants or buildings.

To prepare an area for stone mulch, first remove weeds, roots and all. Rake and tamp the soil and then apply 2–4" of stone mulch. Sometimes I place filter fabric atop the soil before I spread the stones. I pin it with special staples to the ground so it doesn't bunch up and become unsightly.

Please note that filter fabric or landscape fabric lets water through into the soil. As I mentioned earlier, do not use plastic impermeable weed barriers beneath the stones, because this prevents any water from reaching the earth.

The downside of stone mulch is that it can accumulate leaves, which need to be blown off. Also, the leaf matter can settle within the spaces and weed seeds may germinate in this bit of organic material. On the other hand, it makes a great look in a home landscape and does not adversely impact the environment if used in small areas.

Stone mulch is appropriate for plant beds that prefer arid conditions with a sunny aspect. Here, Ed Impara used fine stone mulch to cover a plant bed. Do not use this kind of fine stone mulch on a slope, as it can move.

"Rip Rap" for Retaining Slopes

Rip rap is a general term for rocks that are placed close together on a slope, covering it. Similar to stone mulch, it is used to prevent plant growth and to keep soil from washing down the hill in a rainstorm. Large rocks are often used in rip rap applications because they do not move easily.

You must have a ready supply of rocks in order to create a rip rap slope. You can see rip rap slopes on the sides of highways where they can appear harsh and overwhelming. They are used to minimize lawn mowing and to eliminate the need for planting. Highway rip rap is not a good example, but rip rap slopes can be very appealing, in a rugged sort of way, if done carefully.

How to Create a Rip Rap Slope

Once you have collected your rocks or boulders and have them on site, you are ready to begin. Before placing any stone however, you must prepare the base of the slope. This is very important! Dig a 2'-deep ditch at the bottom of the slope and place the first course of boulders or rocks in it. This is called a "toe ditch" because it is at the toe or base of the slope. The large boulders placed in this ditch support and hold the rip rap slope in place.

After that, cover the slope with geotextile filter fabric. This is done before setting any stones.

A very well done stone rip rap slope at the Steinhardt Garden in Mt. Kisco, New York. These stones have flat sides and are set securely in the slope, almost looking like a slanted wall. The stone channel at the base helps to absorb excess storm water.

A more rustic rip rap slope. The natural stones are placed in a single layer atop filter fabric. A nearby rhododendron hangs over the rocks.

The fabric prevents any undue soil loss beneath the rocks but lets water through. Apply the filter fabric loosely over the ground so as not to puncture it. Make sure that enough fabric extends beyond the edges of the rip rap area so you can fold the fabric under the rocks along the edge. Now place the stones by hand or with an excavator or backhoe.

You may have to move big rocks with a machine because it is so much easier to manipulate them into place. The machine can move a rock with a little nudge here and there to visually improve the end result. A machine rental may be expensive, but you get a lot done in a short time. You can also rent a small skid steer machine or tractor.

Do not add plants to a rip rap slope. It creates a maintenance headache. Rip rap is not a rock garden – it is a ground cover that needs little attention and prevents soil erosion.

* * *

I have talked about sustainable use of stone in this chapter and how their use can help the environment. I touched upon permeable gravel walks, but there is so much more to say about walkways in the landscape! In the next chapter, The Many Faces of a Stone Walk, we take a look at how the addition of a stone walk or path can make a garden exceptional.

Four

The Many Faces of a Stone Walk

~◡

Walk as if you are kissing the Earth with your feet.

~ Thich Nhat Hanh

Most of us see outdoor walks as a fairly straightforward affair. They connect point A to point B, acting as pedestrian links or connectors. But if you think about it, walks and paths also establish the rhythm of an outdoor space. They weave through a landscape and control the speed of our pace by their layout. Curving walks slow us down while straight walks encourage us to move more rapidly.

The paving of a walk also affects our tempo. Walkways covered in loose gravel or small pebbles make us walk a little slower and focus on where we place our feet. We may even listen to the sound of the gravel underfoot. Conversely, we walk a little faster on hard, paved walks, because they offer a more solid footing and we feel more secure. The combination of a walk's look, its materials and how it leads us through a space makes it a dynamic player in the landscape. I hope that this chapter will leave you thinking of new ways to get from point A to point B.

The Many Faces of a Stone Walk

Most of our everyday walks are paved in a predictable pattern. But as we become aware of what is possible and see examples of innovative paving ideas, this is starting to change. Who says that stone paving has to be boring? The walks shown here illustrate some of the ways stone can be used to create an attractive walking surface and add some panache to a garden. These ideas can be used in any size landscape, large or small.

The straight rectilinear lines of stone pavers are interrupted by round natural stones in the United States Botanic Garden in Washington, DC.

Flagstones of varying shapes and sizes make up a mosaic pattern in this walkway. The term flagstone refers to any hard, flat stone slab used for paving.

A walk made up of granite cobblestones, set in an alternating pattern. Cobblestone edging rises above the walk by about 4", adding to its unique appeal. It is in the Silas Mountsier Garden in Nutley, New Jersey, and can be seen through the Garden Conservancy Open Days.

This is the Afternoon Garden at the historic estate Naumkeag, in Stockbridge, Massachusetts, a garden open to the public. The walk features very large pieces of natural stone intermixed with smaller ones and wide joints between them.

Belgian blocks are laid flat in a rectangular shape, mimicking a paver. These groups of Belgian blocks are divided by wide joints filled with good soil and planted with fine-bladed grasses. Notice how the alignment of Belgian blocks alternates in each "rectangle."

A stone walk does not necessarily have to contain only stone. Here, in a walk in Big Sur, California, small natural stones and different-colored bricks are also set in the paving. It is like a mosaic on the ground plane.

Mixing small light-colored irregular natural stones in with others makes for a unique pattern. The moss that grows naturally between the stones is a bonus in this garden walk.

Stone Walk Paving Ideas from Chanticleer, a Pleasure Garden

In Wayne, Pennsylvania, about 30 minutes outside of Philadelphia, there is a world-class public garden called Chanticleer. It is a 35-acre pleasure garden that exemplifies the best of plant and garden design, a study of textures and forms, where even the drinking fountains are sculptural. It is also chock-full of walks and paths that feature artful stone paving ideas using stone tiles, stone blocks and more.

The walks in Chanticleer lead from one intriguing garden to another, each with its own distinctive style. There is the Tennis Court, Ruin, Gravel Garden, Pond Garden, Asian Woods, Bell's Woodland and many more. In one area below the Pond Garden, a wide walk leads to a bridge with distinctive curved wood rails. Along with the bridge, the unique paving also catches the eye. The hard surfaced walk leads to a small section of light gray granite Belgian blocks set in an unusual flared layout. The shape of the block paving and the light stone seem to say, "Come and enjoy this crossing."

This stone "apron" serves as a transition between the wood bridge and walk. Belgian block pavers, fashioned from hard granite, are a good choice for paving here because this walk also serves as a road for utility vehicles. Belgian block handily withstands wear and tear of vehicular traffic.

The curved wood handrails denote a bridge that crosses a small stream in the Chanticleer public garden. The light gray Belgian block embedded in the blacktop road also announce a transition. These subtle but effective visual cues transform what might be an ordinary space into something special.

Another alluring stone walk at Chanticleer, composed of loosely ar ranged rectilinear stones, pieced together in a playful way. There is no mortar between the stones. The soft ostrich ferns *(Matteuccia struthiopteris)* contrast well with the hard paving to create a shady idyll.

Who says garden walks must be fully paved? This walk at Chanticleer is made of crushed stone, granite Belgian blocks and a few natural stones, placed in an almost abstract layout. The open space is as appealing as the paved areas.

This wonderful path in Chanticleer is made of narrow pieces of slate, laid on edge and set in a gravel base. The stones are in alternating rows in a straight running pattern.

Another section of the same slate walk in Chanticleer features a starburst paving pattern. Using stone on edge like this opens a world of possibilities in paving design.

Design Tips for a Stone Walk

Most people make their front walk too narrow. This ends up looking like a cramped strip – a runway to a front door – suitable for only one person. When installing a walk, always err on the wide side. A front walk should be at least 4' wide. This creates direction and unmistakably tells guests to go "this way." It also allows people to walk side by side, and plants can grow over the edges without making the walk less usable.

You can make the walk appear wider by leaving a generous shoulder on one or both sides. This means that the land is somewhat level with the

Punctuate with a Stone Border in the Paving

Punctuation in a paved area is fun, especially when you do it with stone. I like to insert a narrow stone border for a walk or patio because it acts as a trim, bringing a decorative touch to a large expanse. Several rows of Belgian block can be set in a "running bond" pattern to contain the area. It can be two blocks thick or more, depending on how wide a line you want to create.

walk before it slopes down or up. The extra bit of shoulder room makes the walk feel and look wider. Another tip: Make sure a front walk is at least 30" or more away from any walls so people don't brush against a wall as they walk.

Wider walkways work well with larger homes and contemporary style homes. It is not uncommon to make the front walk at least 5–6' wide in a modern setting, making the front yard seem more spacious. A wide entryway can provide room for planters that add some embellishment to the scene. The walk can be made wider with a border row, called a "soldier row," of stones, bricks or pavers.

Walks should be wide enough to accommodate outdoor equipment. For example, a lawn mower or garden cart requires about 4', while a tractor may need 5–6' or more.

A 5'-wide walk is a good width for two people to walk side by side. Note the difference of material along both edges.

The Difference Between a Walk and a Path

We often use the words, "walk" and "path," to mean the same thing, but in landscape design there is a distinction between the two terms. Walks usually serve a particular purpose, like leading to a specific place, such as from a drive to a house. They are also fairly permanent installations and designed for more use, while paths are secondary in importance.

Walks are wider than paths, the average width ranging from 3-1/2–6' – allowing for two people to walk side by side.

Paths are narrower than walks, measuring about 2–3' wide. They accommodate one person and are more informal, typically curving or meandering. They may be paved or covered with loose gravel or mulch.

A good example of a stone path and a stone walk. I designed each to reflect its function.

Choosing the Right Stone for Your Walk

Stone walks offer a wonderful opportunity to display stone paving to its best advantage. With a wide variety to choose from, you want to find the stone that complements your home and can withstand the climate where you live. Here are the three criteria you should consider:

Style: Irregular, rough stones look great with a country house, while the clean lines of smooth, cut stone are suitable for a modern home. Tawny-colored sandstone matches a desert home, and gray-blue bluestone adds character to a colonial style house.

Climate: Dense stone like granite and quartzite can withstand freezing temperatures and is best for cold climates. More porous stones like limestone are better suited to warmer areas, as they absorb water, which could freeze and crack the stone. Ask your stone yard about a stone's freeze/thaw ratings.

Function: For front walks where traffic is high, smooth, uniform stones that are set evenly on a concrete or gravel base are recommended. This lessens the probability of tripping and reduces maintenance. A simple stepping-stone path is better suited for gardens or backyards.

The slip resistance of a stone is also a consideration, particularly in areas where the walk is exposed to the elements. Smooth stone surfaces may become slippery when wet, so most quarries or stone yards will rough up the stone by applying different surface finishes. These give the stone some grip or texture and range from a bushhammered or brushed finish to a thermal finish and others. Always ask about the possible surface treatments available.

I used dark gray cut stones on a concrete base in this walk. The stone is dense and able to tolerate wear and tear. It contrasts beautifully with the rounded green boxwood plants.

Categories of Stone Types for Paving

Paving stone can be either natural or quarried. There are several general categories of stone for paving. These are fieldstone, flagstone or cut stone.

Fieldstone is any uncut stone that is indigenous to an area. It is not quarried. You usually use fieldstone the way it is found, with a minimum of shaping. It is used in settings where a natural stone look is desired.

Flagstone is sedimentary stone that is quarried, has a relatively smooth surface and can be split into thin slabs or "flags." Available in a range of colors, shapes and sizes, flagstone provides a good surface to walk on. The flagstone quarried in Pennsylvania, New York and Connecticut is a durable choice known as bluestone. In Colorado, a popular flagstone is Colorado Buff. In the Southwest, Arizona flagstone, a form of sandstone, is widely used for walks and patios.

Cut Stone is any type of stone that is cut to a dimensional shape. It may be formed into thin pieces or thicker blocks. It is cut to a desired shape either during the quarrying process or installation, and is quite durable.

The following table is a list of common stone types used in landscaping, their characteristics and their typical landscape uses.

If you want to grow plants along your walkway, make the walk at least a foot wider than you think you need. Here, beautiful yellow Japanese forest grass (*Hakonechloa macra aurea*) hangs over a stone path, obscuring it and making it seem narrower than it is.

STONE	DESCRIPTION	APPEARANCE	WHERE IT COMES FROM	COLORS	PROS	CONS
ARIZONA FLAGSTONE (Sandstone)	sedimentary rock formed by layers of cemented sand and tiny rock grains	earthy, tawny look	quarried in Arizona. Ash Fork, Arizona has claimed itself "The Flagstone Capital of the World"	pastel pinks, buff gold, dark red, tan, brown, yellow, gray and white	cooler surface temperatures in summer. Weather resistant. Used in outdoor projects.	porous and tends to be soft. Should be sealed to avoid staining
GRANITE	igneous rock	patterns with fine to coarse grains	Northeast and East Coast of U.S., Texas, South Dakota, Minnesota and others	white, gray, yellow, mauve, pink, crimson, black,	extremely hard surface, high resistance to scratching and acid, amenable to cutting and shaping, good for high traffic areas	costly
QUARTZITE	hard, metamorphic rock	grainy, sandpaper-like surface which becomes glassy, very attractive	Oklahoma, Utah, South Dakota, Central Texas, Wisconsin, Appalachians	white, silver, yellow, gray, various shades of pink and red	resistant to weathering and chemicals. Non-slip surface, resistant to stains	rough, textured surface
BLUESTONE	blue-gray sandstone with quartz	flat with a rough texture. Classical look, usually cut into rectangular and square shapes and is thin	primarily found in Northeast (Pennsylvania and New York)	blue, gray, lilac and burgundy	dense, durable paving, non-slip surface, commonly used as outdoor paving, resistant to freeze-thaw cycles	requires proper sealing to resist chlorine or salt water
LIMESTONE	sedimentary rock composed of calcite	natural split surface, Elegant.	commonly found in Indiana	gray, beige, yellow and black	used outdoors for its aesthetic qualities and ability to be cut into various shapes and sizes. Classic look.	has high absorption – needs to be sealed
TRAVERTINE	form of limestone	pitted holes and troughs in its surface; weathered look. It can be polished to a smooth, shiny finish	found naturally in Oklahoma and Texas	shades of brown, tan, white, cream, gray and coral-red	durable, higher-end stone, stays cool outdoors, used for patios and garden paths	will react to acidic liquids which will result in dulling
BASALT	igneous or volcanic rock, gray basalt building stone of Pacific NW. Bold textures	lightly textured and dark	commonly found in Montana and British Columbia	natural gray, beige or black	used in walls, columns, veneers, stairs, walks, patios	is a porous material and will stain; must seal

Installing a Stone Walk on a Crushed Stone Base

The details for installing a stone walk vary depending on location, weather and more. Check with your local stone yard to get instructions for your specific area. Here is the basic step-by-step process for stone paving on a crushed stone base:

STEP 1: Lay out the walk with string and stakes
The best way to lay out a walk is to mark out the center line with marking paint, a 100' tape measure or string. If the walk is to be straight, you can drive in a stake or rebar in the ground at the

This walk consists of 3' x 3' bluestone pavers set abutting each other to make a solid paved garden walk.

beginning center point, attach string to it and pull a straight, taut line to a stake located at the other end of the walk. To locate the edges of the walk: From this center string line, measure out equally to both left and right sides along the entire length of the walkway. I use marking paint to mark these points and then connect the dots to mark out the walk.

Similarly, if the walk is to be curving, paint out the alignment of the center of the walk on the ground. Then measure out equally from the center line at various points to locate the edges of the path.

STEP 2: Purchase the Materials
Measure the length and width of the walk and determine the square footage of the walk. Order the correct amount of base materials to be delivered to the site. And go to a stone yard to select your desired stone. You may be able to buy the stone on a pallet, which is already sorted to include pavers of the same size and shape. Always buy at least ten percent more stone than you think you need, because sometimes you may choose not to use a certain paver on site or you need to cut some pieces.

STEP 3: Prepare Base
Dig out the soil inside the marked-out edge lines to a depth suitable for your climate. I live in the

snowy Northeast where the ground freezes, so I excavate 9–10" of soil to accommodate 6" of subbase, 2" of base and 1/2–2" for stone. Soil type and climate will determine how deep you dig. In general, figure on a 4–6"-deep excavation in mild-winter climates with well-drained soil. Determine beforehand where you may be able to use the soil generated by this dig and transport it there.

Add edging on the sides to keep stones from spreading apart. If using any kind of edging, install it now.

Rake the soil surface smooth, then lightly dampen the ground and compact the ground with a hand or power tamper. Install Item #4 (also called quarry process) into the excavated area in 1–2"-inch thick layers. Tamp the layer well with a tamper or vibratory plate tamper, then add more and tamp again. This is the most important step – compacting it. You can also use gravel as a subbase as long as you compact it well.

When you have a firm, compacted subbase, spread 2" of stone dust. You can add an optional layer of landscape fabric between the subbase and stone dust to prevent the it from filtering down into the base. Rake the surface smooth. Run a string line (tied to stakes) down the length of the walk to act as a guideline which indicates where the level of the finished surface will be.

STEP 4: Lay the stones
Lay the pavers close together, leaving 1/4–1/2" gaps between them. (The spacing is up to you. This advice is for a closely spaced walk.) If setting the stone in a particular pattern, have that figured out before you start. Tap each stone into the sand with a rubber mallet to set it. Make sure that the stones are level with each other and at the same level as the string line.

STEP 5: Fill the Joints Between the Stones
Sweep the walk and then pile sand or stone dust on the walkway. Using a sweeper brush or broom, sweep sand or stone dust into the joints between stones. Spray it down with a fine spray of water. Add more filler into the joints and wet it again if necessary. Make sure the joints are completely filled with sand. A good suggestion is to use polymeric sand in the joints.

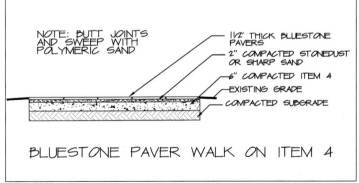

NOTE: BUTT JOINTS AND SWEEP WITH POLYMERIC SAND

1½" THICK BLUESTONE PAVERS
2" COMPACTED STONEDUST OR SHARP SAND
6" COMPACTED ITEM 4
EXISTING GRADE
COMPACTED SUBGRADE

BLUESTONE PAVER WALK ON ITEM 4

Typical stone paver walk set on a compacted Item #4 base (known as quarry process, QP, crusher run or similar) and a compacted stone dust setting bed. Some people use sharp sand for the setting bed instead of stone dust. Your stone supplier can give you advice.

Installing a stone walk: the bluestone edging is in place and the subbase materials are piled on the walk prior to being spread. We used an Item #4 (quarry process, QP, crusher run or similar) for a subbase. The finished walk is paved in a "crazy" or mosaic pattern where irregular shaped stones are fitted together in a random fashion. Crazy paving is a good choice for curved areas. Here, the pattern provides visual relief from a strong linear walk.

Fill Narrow Joints Between Stones with Polymeric Sand

Polymeric sand, or sand mixed with polymers, is a granular material used between narrow joints in stone paving in walks and patios. The chemical binder swells when it gets wet and ties the sand particles together to prevent weeds from growing in the joints and diminish any washouts during rainstorms. It also stands up to blowers. Overall, polymeric sand improves the durability and stability of a paved surface. It is fast becoming the preferred choice for use as a joint filler between stones.

When polymeric sand is inserted between stones, water has less opportunity to seep into the sand and/or crushed stone below, keeping the base and subbase of paving drier and less likely to move.

If you have wide joints between stones there are similar products you can use. Ask your stone supplier for recommendations.

Japanese Garden Paths

Garden walks, more than any other landscape feature, affect our experience of an outdoor space. Nowhere is this better illustrated than in traditional Japanese tea gardens, where the path serves as a quiet way to take a visitor out of the everyday world. The path is called a *roji*, which means "passageway," "path" or "path ground." This multi-use word indicates the importance of paths in Japanese gardens where they are used to lead through a sequence of areas, each bestowing a different feeling upon the visitor.

The paving patterns of traditional Japanese paths follow certain design principles and are an art form in themselves. I have always been awed by the variations in Japanese paving. Stones are placed with careful irregularity to create a feeling of serenity. This asymmetry encourages your eyes to travel freely around the scene.

In a Japanese garden, the paving style changes as you travel through hidden bends and stopping points. Each new pattern silently signals that you are entering a different area of the landscape. This change can occur where there is an alteration in the ground level, a turn or intersection, or at a portal such as a gate or arbor. At each of these junctures you may choose to pause, reflect or discover something new.

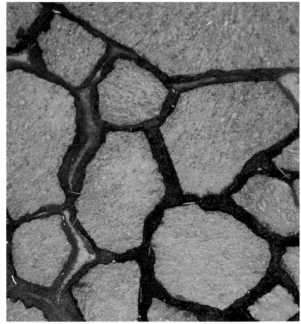

Close-up of a walk in the Japanese Garden in Portland, Oregon, illustrating the attention to detail in their stone paving. The dark mortar between the small stones looks like a thick black outline.

In traditional Japanese gardens, a short, paved section of a path is often installed at a point where the path comes upon a view. Walking on a rustic path, a person normally watches where they step, but once they step onto a paved section of path, it is natural for them to raise their head and see the scenery in front of them. Thus, by manipulating the surface of the walk you can influence how people experience a garden.

The stone paving at the Portland Japanese Garden is fitted together in a carefully crafted arrangement, with no acute angles. The shapes of the stone are irregular but pleasing and come in varying sizes. The inclusion of a large stone within a sea of smaller ones is a feature of Japanese paving.

In some instances, rectangular pieces of cut granite are combined with natural stones and stepping stones to create unusual layouts. This interplay of right angles and random stone forms creates an artful dialogue between the walker's feet and the paving. Sometimes two long rectangular stones are set parallel to each other or slightly offset in the middle of a path. These smooth granite blocks have been used in tea gardens for centuries and are called "poem card stones" after the strips of paper that poems and prayers are written on.

The visual variety that these stones insert into a paving pattern is engaging. The mortar used sometimes has ground charcoal mixed with it to darken the color of the spaces in between. The paving is a work of art that you can walk on...a celebration of flat stone in all its glory. It is a paving pattern we can emulate in our stone walks.

Stepping Stone Paths

A stepping stone path is a casual way to explore a garden, leading from one area to the next. It's also practical because its narrow scale can fit into plants beds to let you weed and plant. Stepping stone paths are easy to install, but before you start, you should consider the many forms such a path can take.

Stepping stones appear in various shapes in gardens. Some are natural while others are worked to form shapes like rectangles and circles. The stones may be set about 4" apart and about 2" high, but this can vary widely based on individual taste.

The basic stepping stone path consists of stones set in a single file. If you install this kind of path, make sure they are large enough for a person's foot (not too small!) and are smooth enough so one doesn't trip. And, of course, the spacing of the stones should match your stride. Next, consider the area around the stones; you can place them in a field of reddish-brown mulch or you can place them singly in a light-colored crushed stone walk (as shown). The contrast of the gray stone with the crushed stone works well to attract the eye and show people where to step.

Natural stones, used as stepping stones, are set to match the cadence of normal footsteps. This is measured as the distance between the heel of one foot to the other. This is in the Ed Merrin garden.

Variety in Stepping Stone Paths

There are many ways to use stone in a stepping stone path in the garden – from formal to rustic. The color, type, shape and layout of the stones contribute to the overall look.

Replacing One Stepping Stone Walk with Another: Which Do You Prefer?

One of my clients decided that he wanted to replace the walk shown here with a more free-form stepping stone path. He wanted it to look less formal and more gardenesque – so he removed the rectangular bluestone pavers and replaced them with flat, native path stone set in a loose arrangement. Each of these stepping stone walks leading to the sliding glass doors has its strengths. The one on the left appears more formal while the one on the right has character.

The rectangular bluestone pavers are set about 3" apart, making them easy to walk on. Boxwood is planted alongside the path, leading the eye, and the visitor, straight to the door.

The walk was replaced with natural path stones set a little farther apart in a free flowing stepping stone pattern. The boxwood was replaced with lawn to create more space around the path.

Ten Tips for Setting a Stepping Stone Path

1. The size of a stone for one step is 12" wide.
2. The size of a stone for two feet on the stone is about 24" wide.

A stepping stone path in the Japanese Garden of the Cleveland Botanic Garden illustrates the design tips for setting stone in a Japanese-inspired path.

3. Use larger flat stones, 36" wide or more, near a house or structure. These act as landings and can be squared off, in a more formal style.
4. Mix rectangular stones and stones with rounded corners in longer runs to create interest. Also, change the sizes so that they are not all the same.
5. Flat stones that are a circular shape can be placed in a long run of stepping stones to add a little punch.
6. Space the small stepping stones to match the spacing of your normal footsteps – remember the ordinary right-left walking gait when you do this. Step on them in several practice runs before installing!
7. The height of the stones should be set about 2" above ground. This can be altered at the discretion of the gardener.
8. Stagger the arrangement with 4 stones in a line and then the next 3 stones set slightly to the side.
9. For variation, mix medium-sized rectangular stones staggered with small stones placed close together in between.
10. Angle the stones slightly along the walk. Angling creates interest.

The Therapeutic Benefits of Reflexology Paths

You might want to consider an upraised pebble path as a way to experience a therapeutic foot "massage." The pressure on the bottom of your feet is akin to the practice of reflexology, an ancient healing art. Walking on paths made from rounded pebbles applies pressure to the soles of your feet and toes, said to relieve symptoms in other parts of the body. This is based on the idea that the nerves in your feet correspond with organs such the lungs, liver and kidneys. Walking on reflexology paths is said to induce a relaxation effect and reduce anxiety. It may work so well because our feet contain greater than 7,000 nerves, more nerve endings than any other part of the body!

Reflexology paths are not yet common in the United States, but are growing in popularity in Asia. In fact, Singapore has reflexology paths in their public gardens. The winding paths shown in the next 4 photos are constructed of small, smooth, rounded pebbles embedded in mortar, set in intriguing decorative patterns. Some stones are thick and rounded, others are thinner to provide strong stimulation to the feet.

The beauty of this kind of path is that you can control the length of your walk, which, in turn affects how much pressure your feet receive. For example, some walks feature smooth stones in lovely swirling patterns with a band of thinner, sharper edged stones next to it, allowing you to take short, light walks on sharper stones and longer walks on adjacent rounded, smooth stones.

A beautiful stone path in the Singapore Botanic Gardens invites you to take off your shoes and walk on the stones.

According to traditional Chinese theory, regularly walking on reflexology paths does the following:

- Stimulates pressure points in your feet that correspond to major body organs and areas.
- Stimulates vital energy and blood flow throughout your body.
- Relieves stress, improves balance, enhances physical and mental well-being.

With all these benefits, it sure seems like a good idea to add these unique and beautiful stone paths to our gardens and public parks! You can find installation guides for reflexology paths online. It is similar to creating a mosaic pebble path.

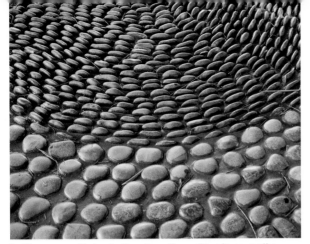

In Singapore Botanic Gardens the reflexology paths are comprised of different shaped stones in swirling patterns. You may choose to walk on the stones set pointed side up for a stimulating walk or step onto the smoother stones for something a little less jarring.

The rounded pebbles are set upright in this portion of a reflexology path to provide a brisk massage on the soles of bare feet.

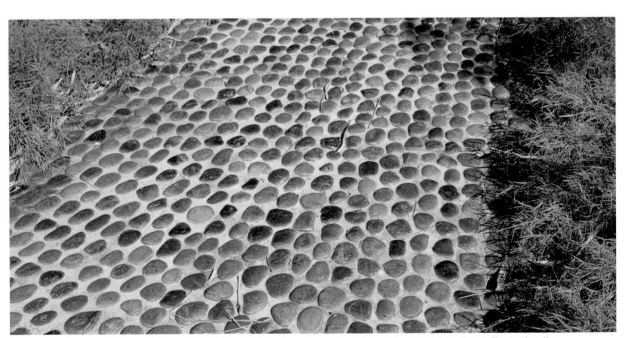

Smooth water-rounded pebbles, set flat into a light-colored mortar base, are easy to walk on. They give the soles of bare feet a very soothing massage. Visually, the contrast of the dark stones and light mortar makes this walk appealing.

Lotusland – A Colorful Pebble Mosaic

Another kind of pebble path can be found in Lotusland, a public garden in Montecito, California. It features elaborate mosaics in a swirling carpet of multi-colored pebbles. It was commissioned by property owner Madame Ganna Walska, designed by Jim Minah and installed by stonemason Oswald Da Ros in 1969.

Tawny-colored pebbles of varying hues, create a swirling abstract pattern.

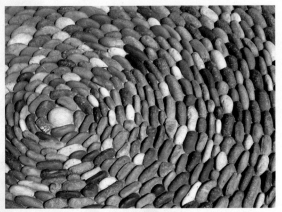

The colors of the small stones are mixed in this radial pattern. The white pebbles stand out among the reddish brown ones and draw the eye around in a circular motion. The central stone is a larger white one.

*   *   *

Stone walks often lead to garden steps. The options for outdoor steps are numerous. These can be in the form of boulder steps, stone treads, grass steps using stone, gravel steps or more. The next chapter explores some of the outdoor step choices available in the world of stone.

Five

Garden Steps Steal the Show

~)

Nature first, second and third – architecture after awhile.
~ Calvert Vaux

Stone steps in a garden really do steal the show. They are the "architecture" in a landscape and provide the drama of a change in elevation. No matter their style or appearance, your eye cannot help but follow the steps up or down. They act as a focal point and compel you to follow their lead.

You can take any sloped garden and make it more accessible with a few stone steps. Stone is a natural choice for landscape steps; it is durable, weatherproof, extremely long-lasting and adds a timeless appearance. There is a wealth of design options and material choices for stone steps in a landscape. This chapter looks at some of the possibilities. In all cases, the result is the same: steps add magic to a landscape.

Boulder steps are useful in remote garden areas. Note the beautiful fall colors of the dwarf 'Mt. Airy' *Fothergilla*, a native cultivar, on the right. I planted it as an accent to the dark gray stone.

The Rustic Call of Boulder Steps

A slope can be transformed into a showstopper by the addition of a few rustic boulder steps and a variety of plants. Large, flat, natural rocks placed atop each other are a great way to create steps, add interest and provide a little bit of adventure to those nimble enough to climb them. These are not the kind of steps you might use as an entry to a house or in any area where there is a lot of traffic, because you must watch carefully where you put your feet. In addition, they are not safe to use in wet, snowy or icy conditions. You should add handrails for safety. However, they are a rustic hillside solution for little-used areas or where they may serve as a view from a house or porch.

Use boulder steps where their rough appearance fits with the rest of the landscape. Rough stone steps are suited for non-important, secondary passageways – in remote areas, up a rocky hill or in a wooded slope. There is an adage that says the type of stone step you build should be appropriate to how it is used. The next pages show the process for installing boulder steps.

1. **Determine how many boulder steps you will need**

First, consider how many steps you will need to get from point A at the top down to point B at the bottom. An easy way to determine the rise or vertical drop is to use a straight wooden board, a tape measure and a carpenter's level. Lay the board horizontally at the top of the slope, where the top step will be, and place the carpenter's level atop it. Once the board is level, use the tape measure to find the distance from the ground up to the bottom of the board – the height is equal to the steps you need to install. For example, if you measure the height to be 18" and you figure you will have 6"-high stones, then you will need 3 stones. Generally, individual outdoor steps feel comfortable when they are between 5" and 7" high.

Stones that have edges that slope inward allow rainwater to fall straight down off the step. Make sure to slightly pitch the boulder step forward to facilitate drainage.

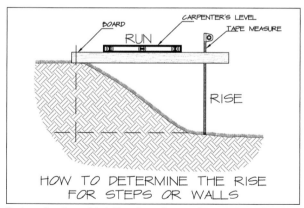

HOW TO DETERMINE THE RISE FOR STEPS OR WALLS

Determine how high the rise of your slope is by using a tape measure, carpenter's level and a straight board.

You can also do this with a simple line level (this is a small level attached to a string). Tie one end of the string to a stake that is flush in the ground where the top step will be located. Now go stand at the bottom step location and hold the string horizontally taut, adjusting it up or down until it reads level.

The run of these boulder steps passes through a shady area but opens up in the daylight at the top, with the top step. The light draws people upward.

2. **Find the right natural stones to use as steps**

   Next, you must find the proper rocks to use as steps. You may find them from the site or, more likely, you can visit a stone yard or quarry and choose the flat boulders you think are appropriate. Choose large pieces with a relatively flat side for use as steps. The steps should all have a similar thickness. This is a time-consuming chore, but it is well worth the effort!

3. **Excavate the base of the first step and fill with fine crushed stone**

   Pick the stone that you want for your first step. Dig a hole into the base of the slope that is large enough to fit the first stone and lay a 12"-deep layer of crushed stone. I also suggest that you install a woven geotextile fabric in the bottom of the hole before you install the stone. This prevents the stone from sinking into the soil beneath.

   When you fill, add a little more crushed stone toward the back of the hole to make the stone pitch very slightly forward (1/4" per foot) to promote drainage. By pitching the base forward the water runs out, away from the steps. Tamp the crushed stone by placing a short piece of 2" x 4" lumber against the stone and hitting it firmly with a rubber mallet. Do this repeatedly on the entire surface until the base is well compacted. Place your large flat stone on top and check with a carpenter's level that it sits level from side to side and is slightly pitched forward. You can adjust the stone by altering the depth of the setting bed to make it sit higher or lower. You can also place the piece of lumber on the step and pound it down again with the mallet to make it sit lower.

These rough stone steps are not meant to be an everyday walkway but show off the plants nicely. Evergreen pachysandra (Pachysandra terminalis) is a good groundcover for the partial shady conditions here. It grows easily among rocks and spreads to soften the look of the boulders.

4. Lay second step partially atop first step and continue

Now that your first step is in place, dig back into the bank from the top of your first step and repeat the process for the next stone. This step sits on a tamped crushed stone base but also is partially atop the first step. You determine how much to overlap the first step, depending on the stone's size and shape. It is not an exact science when working with boulder steps, but remember to leave at least 12" of stone visible to act as a step tread.

5. Soften the sides with plantings

The key to beautiful rustic stone steps is to blend them into the hillside. Sometimes they are meant to show off plants more than to act as a passageway. Add good quality topsoil to the sides of the stones and plant it with interesting small plants such as yellow creeping Jenny, Japanese forest grass or sedum. Check out some suggestions for plants in Chapter 8, Plants and Stone. Rocks placed along the side of the steps help form the perfect spot for displaying plants.

Chiseled stone slabs are set on top of each other to climb a rise to a large level play area. I planted tall ornamental grass such as maiden grass *(Miscanthus sinensis gracillimus)* as a tall divider between the upper and lower areas.

Stone Slab Steps – A Wonderful Choice

If you want an informal and natural set of steps but with a bit more consistency than rustic boulder steps, consider installing stone slab steps. They are my favorite kind of garden steps, because they add just the right amount of formality and are easier to walk on. Stone slabs are fabricated in the quarry and have fairly uniform thicknesses to ensure comfortable and safe walking conditions.

With a wide variety available, you can choose slabs that are manufactured from bluestone, granite, sandstone, limestone and more. You can combine these slab risers with a gravel or fieldstone tread for a wonderful effect. You can also have them sit one atop the other. And you can inset them between two walls or have no side walls at all. The step design possibilities are numerous.

Step Tread and Riser Dimensions

We have all walked up steps that felt odd to walk on – they were either too low and you felt like taking giant steps to walk on them two at a time, or they were too steep and you had to hold on to something as you climbed them. Outdoor steps must have the appropriate tread depth and riser height to feel comfortable and to be safe.

So, what are the right size outdoor steps? Well, for one thing, they are not like indoor steps! Outdoor steps are generally lower and deeper than those inside a house. Steps are made up of the tread, the horizontal portion that you step on, and the riser, the vertical portion of the step. It's important to have the correct ratio of tread-to-rise. In general, the shorter the rise, the bigger the tread. A guideline that is commonly used to establish the tread riser dimensions is the following formula:

Twice the riser height
plus the tread depth should equal 26" or 27"

$$2R + T = 26" \text{ or } 27"$$

The dimensions of the treads and risers in outdoor steps are related: as the dimension of one becomes greater, the dimension of the other becomes smaller. Do not make an outdoor step lower than 4" high or less than 12" in depth.

The installation instructions are similar to boulder steps – they must sit on a sturdy base of crushed stone or gravel. For a standard stone upon stone step layout, start the first step on relatively level ground, just before the slope begins. The first slab may be a little larger than the others to act as a landing of sorts. Overlap each stone by a few inches, but make sure to leave at least 12" of tread

Here I used 9"x9" bluestone slabs with a chiseled rock face as the step riser.

area, preferably a little more. If the slabs are not exactly level, you can use small pieces of stone to shim the treads level, side to side. The back of the top tread should end just below the crest of the slope, because it looks a little better when the top step is slightly lower than top of the hill.

You can find stone slabs at a local stone supply yard. Often, stone is sold by weight, but many times, good stepping stones are sold individually. If your stoneyard does have stone in bulk, dig around the pile to pick out your favorites. When you choose the slabs, make sure they are without cracks or marks. Touch the surface to determine if it is suitably rough for adequate traction. Don't forget to purchase enough slabs to ensure that you have a sufficient quantity for your steps. And finally, don't let someone else pick out the stones for you and then deliver them without your approval – you should check them out at the supply yard.

Sandstone treads atop fieldstone risers. The treads are dense, fine-grained and have a lovely pinkish cast. They make graceful steps. The 'Anthony Waterer' spirea on the left hides a portion of the walk, encouraging visitors to explore.

Tread and Riser Steps

A common outdoor step style consists of a single stone tread that slightly overhangs a step riser. This kind of step differs from boulder or slab steps in that it features two separate elements: the tread that you step on and the vertical riser. It has a more formal appearance and is suitable for use as front entry steps or wherever there is a lot of foot traffic.

You can choose step treads from a variety of stone materials such as granite, bluestone, limestone, sandstone and marble. Whatever material you choose, the tread must be without chips or cracks and be relatively smooth. You can buy tread stones in various thicknesses. Like other steps, you will want a slight pitch toward the front of the step so that rainwater drains off. In a tread and riser step, you need a pitch of about 1/8" per foot.

A prominent detail in this style of step is the tread overhang. This is distance that a step tread

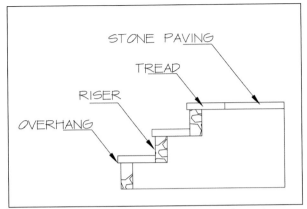

Here is a simple step diagram denoting a stone riser and tread layout.

- Outdoor step risers must be fairly uniform and no higher than 7".
- The landing length should be 36" or more between runs of steps.
- Install a handrail on any elevation change of 18" or greater (important!).
- Pitch the steps forward to ensure surface water drains off.
- A single step is dangerous because people do not expect it. It can become a tripping hazard. Create two steps, instead of one.
- Illuminate outdoor steps with pathlights, or use overhead lights.

extends beyond the riser. An overhang helps to deflect water from running down the face of a riser and adds a nice shadow to the appearance of the step. The tread can overhang the riser by 1 – 1-1/2" depending on the size of the tread and riser and the look you want.

The building of a set of masonry steps for stone treads and risers can become quite involved for the do-it-yourselfer. Keep in mind that the bottom riser must be set on a firm foundation or the steps will be susceptible to settling or frost movement. You must excavate below frost level in your area and fill the area with angular drainage gravel. You can build a rough base from concrete blocks for the steps. There are great YouTube videos that illustrate how to build a base for tread and riser steps.

The tread steps here show how steps can be bordered with a wall (the upper steps) or can stand alone (the lower steps). Note the path lights by the lower steps – steps should always be illuminated at night for safety.

Important: Handrails on Outdoor Steps

Handrails are necessary for outdoor steps. A handrail is a horizontal or sloping rail intended for grasping by the hand for guidance or support. It offers safety and security, especially when it is wet or icy. Towns and municipalities require railings on outdoor steps depending on where they are located and how many steps there are. The final authority on how high the railing should be, and when and where hand railings are required on steps and landings, rests with your local building code official. You must check with them before designing or building any outdoor steps. Safety is of the utmost importance when adding outdoor steps to a landscape.

Going Up, Going Down

If you think about it, we tend to go faster when we descend steps. It is a natural thing to do, and we also pay more attention to our feet, making sure we tread more carefully. Knowing that we have a tendency to look down as we descend steps, pay attention to the stone paving patterns on or near the ground. Also, as you build the steps, think about what you can plant at the bottom of the descent. Sometimes, the descent to the bottom of some steps can lead to a feeling of entering a grotto. To create a grotto impression, plant shrubs with broad leaves on both sides along the bottom steps or have the canopy of nearby trees hang over the base of the steps. A mass planting of large-leaved hostas or wide evergreen shrubs can also do the trick.

Conversely, as we ascend steps, we go more slowly and look up. So, think about what is at the top of the steps. Is it a tree we can set our sights on? Or a bench? You can recreate a mountain top feeling here and offer a view of some sort, and perhaps have a large rock to sit on once you get there.

Plant low growing plants like cranberry cotoneaster (*Cotoneaster apiculatus*) near steps. People notice things near the ground as they descend steps.

The All-Important Edge of Step Treads

The first thing you notice when you look at a set of tread and riser steps is the edges of the step treads. This is because they protrude out beyond the risers to catch our attention. There are several ways that edges can be treated and you must choose which one you prefer when designing or building outdoor steps. When the tread is initially created at the quarry, the stone is cut with a diamond blade or wire saw to produce a clean, saw-cut edge. A sawn finish is raw and harsh and may show the saw marks and other imperfections. It is not a particularly attractive edge, so quarries and stone fabricators treat exposed edges of a step tread stone in several ways:

This 2"-thick step tread has a thermal finish on the edge, a fieldstone riser and over-hangs the riser by 1-1/2". The overall look is clean and inviting. Handrails were installed af-ter this photo was taken – you must install these for safety.

Flamed or thermal edge – The face of the saw-cut edge is torched with a high temperature flame producing a rough-textured and slip-resistant finish. This is called a flamed or thermal finish. It is commonly used on outdoor paving stones, both on top surfaces and exposed edges, to produce a pebbled texture. It is a common step edge treatment.

Rock face – The edge is chiseled by hand to give the stone a more distinct, rustic appearance. There are conspicuous indentations that catch the light to create noticeable shadows. This unique edge treatment is a centuries old technique that provides a natural look.

Full bullnose – If you like a formal, rounded over edge, then bull nose is the edge for you. This edge is thermal-treated after being rounded on the top and bottom of the stone.

Snapped edge – This refers to a natural breaking of a stone either by hand or machine. The break is at right angles to the top and bottom surface and features irregular edge details and random undulations that look like the natural quarry texture.

A step tread with a chiseled rock face edge creates a more rustic feel. Here the risers are granite blocks. 'All Gold' Japanese forest grass *(Hakonechloa macra 'All Gold')* adds a bright yellow touch.

The rounded form of a full bullnose edge adds a formal and elegant touch to any masonry project. There is also a half-bullnose (also called a waterfall edge), which is rounded on the top only.

Rounded Steps Invite and Delight

We all enjoy the look of rounded steps in a garden. They may not be suited for a front entry, where straightforward steps are easier to climb, but the organic curved shape is perfectly suited for a romantic outdoor setting. The appeal of rounded stone steps comes from the contrast of a soft shape and a hard material. The curve adds a gentleness to the scene, even though the steps are made from durable stone. The shape hints at elegant aspirations and evokes a sense of anticipation.

Gertrude Jekyll, the pioneer English garden designer and writer (1843–1932), endorsed curved steps and urged people to make the step treads wide and the risers low "so that they are easy-going" (from *Gardens for Small Houses* by Gertrude Jekyll and Sir Lawrence Weaver). This is an apt phrase for the effect that rounded steps have on the landscape: they flow out and encourage visitors to move through the garden in an "easy-going" manner.

If you want to create a memorable garden, consider inserting a few rounded stone steps. They endow a landscape with mystery; even when the plants are dormant, sleeping in the chilled ground, the stone curves remain.

The key to rounded steps is to know the radius of the curve and give this information to the stone supplier. They can cut the step treads in whatever radius you want. Rounded steps allow people to flare out in any direction.

Gentle Curved Steps

I find that rounded steps outdoors look better if they are lower and wider than normal steps. The low profile enhances their flowing appearance. They do not have to be perfectly semicircular but can simply bow out in the middle. The more gentle the curve, the better!

Here is how you begin any project: lay it out on the ground to ensure it works on the site.

Steps fashioned from fieldstone are well suited for garden settings. The fieldstones are mortared together and follow all the same recommendations for the tread and riser dimensions. I especially love fieldstone steps that are in a curved layout, because the rough fieldstone is an unlikely material for such a genteel feature.

The finished product. Rounded steps can be constructed from fieldstone as shown here. The ivy on the wall softens the stone and makes this entrance all the more inviting. The large upper step offers room for small pots of flowers.

Grass Steps: A Personal Favorite

Grass treads are my favorite kind of garden step. I saw them for the first time in the 1970s in Dumbarton Oaks in Washington, D.C., a public garden designed by Beatrix Farrand. I was captivated by the simplicity and functionality of grass steps and have used them in my landscapes ever since. They add a quiet sense of ceremony to any outdoor setting and hark back to the grassed treads of classic English gardens. But this kind of step can be used in all manner of settings, from cottage gardens to contemporary landscapes, which is why they are so popular.

The treads for grass steps are turfgrass. The risers are constructed from stone (or corten steel or concrete). Stone risers can be fashioned from granite Belgian blocks, bluestone or limestone pavers set upright, thin granite edging or fieldstone. They must have a suitable base, such as a concrete footing, so that they do not move. And the treads, since they are grass, must be pitched more than normal stone steps so that the water runs off before the grass gets too soggy. Make the back of the grass tread higher than the front – I recommend a pitch of at least 1/4" per foot forward (or more).

The beauty of grass steps is their versatility. They can be formed to be straight lines or be laid out as curved steps. They can butt up to a wall, blend into the surrounding lawn or be edged with rocks.

Simple grass steps fashioned from fieldstone found on site are an accent that fits with any style garden.

Here, slightly bowed grass steps with risers made from split Belgian blocks end at a curved stone wall. It is important to pitch each step up so rain drains off. Mow the steps with a string trimmer. I planted lady's mantle (*Alchemilla mollis*) atop the wall.

They can be straight lines that fan out as they climb a slope. They can be made to be long treads that cut across a hill, creating a ceremonial feel. Best of all, they are relatively inexpensive to build!

The depth of the grass treads can vary from 18–36" or more. Just make sure to maintain a pitch down to the front of the treads. And remember, the deeper the tread, the lower the riser. I like to make the treads deeper if I can because the grass thrives with more space between the risers.

Grass steps are well suited for steep slopes, as shown in figure xx. In all, 18 step risers were necessary to scale the hill. I divided them into 3 sets of 6 steps interspersed with 2 wide grass landings. I have found that 6 steps are about the most steps people will ascend outdoors before they look for a landing to stop at. This is a generalization, but it is a handy guide.

I angled the top set of steps to vary the look – the two lower sets of steps are in alignment, creating the effect of a grand outdoor staircase. The effect is very ceremonial. In fact, there was an outdoor wedding, and these grass steps took the place of the aisle!

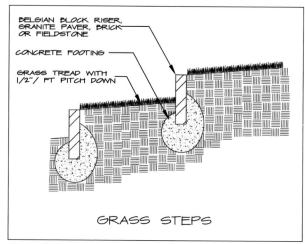

GRASS STEPS

Grass steps need good, well-draining topsoil and a slight pitch forward for continued health of the turf. Make sure not to add too much mortar behind the riser.

These curved grass steps blend in with the lawn, making the lawn appear larger than it is. Stone steps impose themselves and can make a lawn area look smaller.

The curved grass steps shown here are constructed from Belgian blocks. The back of the steps are higher than the front, providing the required pitch necessary for good drainage.

You may assume that you need a slope or hill in order to insert some steps, but that is not necessarily true. You can add soil and create a slight rise and add some steps. In the landscape shown, I added these grass steps and backfilled behind them with soil to make it appear as a natural slope.

* * *

Steps naturally go together with walls. The next chapter, Stone Walls and More, looks at the many ways you can build and use low stone walls in a garden. Stone walls add character while performing many functions. They are the beautiful, useful bones of a landscape.

Six

Stone Walls and More

~

Something there is that doesn't love a wall...
~ Robert Frost

Stone walls add a timeless touch and an earthy richness to any garden. They are multifunctional – you can use a wall to frame a garden, retain a slope or be a freestanding accent. The natural stones, stacked or mortared together, appear as a mosaic of rocky faces creating a wide variety of looks. They may be rounded or blocky, fractured or smooth, depending on what is available and what the stone wall maker chose to use. Many small stones in a wall make it appear intricate and detailed. Large, angular rocks create an imposing, massive look. Weathered, lichen-covered fieldstone, with moss and ferns rooted in the crevices, creates a wall of the softest kind. Once you notice these differences, you will see that a stone wall is indeed a visual dance of stone. After a while, you may begin to see stone walls as art pieces in their own right and become a wall aficionado, appreciating them wherever you go.

Rounded stones protrude out from a retaining wall in The Huntington in San Marino, California. The bumpy look reflects the bold, bright green forms of the plants planted atop the wall.

Besides the type of stone used, the appearance of a wall depends on how it is constructed. There are two general wall building techniques: (1) a wall can be mortared and set on a concrete footing, or (2) the stones can be carefully fitted together without the benefit of any adhesive – called dry stone. Dry stone is one of the oldest construction techniques in the world.

The various colors of the natural stone used in this low freestanding wall make it eye-catching. Who says stones have to be gray?

Once you start noticing landscape walls you will see how many ways they differ. It all depends on the type of stone used, the method of construction, and the intended look. Masonry is an art form.

A dry wall has no mortar between the stones. Here is one with a rustic gate made from tree saplings at the Steinhardt Garden in Mt. Kisco, New York. Note the threshold stone beneath the gate and how it is used as a base for the corner stones.

The Enduring Legacy of Dry Stone Walls

Historically, when rocks were unearthed by farmers' plows, it was natural to stack them on a property line to act as a stone fence. These dry stone walls, built with no mortar or cement, were clear markers, and in some cases, effective barriers, keeping livestock in and intruders out. You can still see our predecessors' rugged dry stone walls bordering fields, woods and roadways. They are a potent visual reminder of a different way of life, when fieldstones were moved with heavy labor and maybe a horse, winch and rock sled. Their presence is emblematic of certain regions – Kentucky horse farm country, Pennsylvania farmland or the New England countryside.

Also called dry stack, dry set or dry laid, these walls, with stones fitted and balanced on top of each other like a puzzle, are remarkably durable and stand for eons if properly built. They also utilize local materials and do not require a deep footing. This means that the wall rises and falls with the earth when frost forms and expands in the soil. The walls, if correctly built, are knitted together so well that they do not fall apart due to frost heave or even earthquakes! They are easily repaired, require a minimum of tools to build and resist fire and water. What else could you ask for in a wall?

In the United States, dry stone structures have a rich historical heritage. In the past, stones were carefully collected and used to build stone dwellings, barns and churches, all without the benefit of mortar. Today, there are groups dedicated to reviving, preserving and promoting the art and craft of dry stack masonry, such as The Dry Stone Conservancy, located in Lexington, Kentucky. In 1996, the Conservancy began a program of apprenticeships in dry stone walling that continues today. Hundreds of people have participated in their programs,

competitions and symposiums. Now, there are trained professional dry stone masons who can build this specific kind of wall, thanks to this organization. If you would like to know more, go to their website, www.drystone.org. In Canada, there is the group called Dry Stone Walling Across Canada: www.dswa.ca. And in the UK, you can go to the Dry Stone Walling Association of Great Britain, whose web address is www.dswa.org.uk.

A historic ruin of a gristmill built around 1800 by Captain Thomas Amis near Rogersville, Tennessee, shows how dry stone walls can pass the test of time. The carefully fitted stone walls are a testament to the skillful masons that built them.

Ten Tips for Building a Freestanding Dry Stone Wall

If you want to try your hand at building a dry stack stone wall, the first thing to do is to study an existing wall to understand some of the intricacies involved. Better yet, there are workshops that you can attend to learn how to master the craft. It requires knowledge and precision to do it correctly. Here are a few general tips:

1. **Choose angular or blocky stones**
   The best stones to use in a dry stack wall are angular or flat. These are better than rounded stones, which are tougher to stack. Angular stones fit together or nest, creating small joints, and actually become stronger as the wall settles. This is because a dry stack wall depends on the force of gravity and friction for its strength and durability. Use rocks that are not too small – the bigger the better.

2. **Create a shallow footing**
   A properly built dry stack wall requires a footing of one course of stone that is buried beneath ground level. Set these stones on a 2"-deep layer of crushed stone for leveling. There is no need to create an elaborate footing, since no mortar is used to bond the stones together. The height of the wall will determine the depth of the footing; a taller wall may require a deeper footing to support it.

Important! Check with your local municipality for any restrictions on the height of a wall that can be built without a permit or engineer's seal. Call or visit your local town or city office before you embark on any wall building!

3. **Build the wall on native soil**
   The base of the wall should be set on native soil, not soil that has been brought in to fill an area. Native soil is less likely to move around and it provides a stable base.

4. **Overlap the joints**
   Avoid continuous horizontal or vertical joints by overlapping stones as much as possible. Long, uninterrupted seams will weaken a wall. Follow the stoneworker's adage: "One stone over two, two stones over one."

5. **Use tie-through stones**
   These are stones that go all the way through the wall to help bind it together. They should be spaced regularly throughout the wall to improve the stability of your wall.

6. **Always pitch stones toward the center of the wall**
   Be sure your stones either lie flat or pitch inward. If they pitch outward, the stones on top of them may slide outward and destroy the wall. Fill the center of the wall with rubble and pebbles.

7. **Allow water to drain through the stones**

   A dry stack wall allows water to drain naturally through the joints between stones. This relieves excess water pressure in the wall.

8. **End the wall well**

   Because the ends of a dry stone wall are more visible and get bumped more often, long tie-through stones or large angular stones should be used here. This gives the end a more finished appearance and a little more stability. You can even taper it down so the wall slopes down to its end.

9. **Choose capstones in advance**

   Capstones are slabs large enough to span the top of a wall and heavy enough to exert downward pressure to help hold the top of the wall together. They also keep out moisture to eliminate frost damage. Capstones should be about the same thickness. Often, they are culled from stone piles and reserved for the final tier and at gates and corners.

10. **Use chinks sparingly**

    After the wall is complete, fill any cracks in the face of the wall with small slivers of stone or stone chips to help tighten it. These are

A dry laid stonewall made from rectangular cut stone in the Native Garden in the New York Botanical Garden exhibits many of the design tips suggested for these types of walls. Note how well it contrasts with the fine leaved grasses behind it.

called chinks or shims. They are necessary because no stone lies completely flat, and some stones may wobble. Broad, flat shims set within the wall stabilize the stone and increases its structural integrity. But do not rely on too many chinks; use them only where they are needed.

Use Remnant Stone for Your Dry Stack Wall

Stone can be hard to find and expensive to buy. Sometimes you can find stone leftovers at a local home supply, big box or garden supply store. These various and sundry pieces, when placed together in a low dry wall, can be your natural backyard accent.

"Batter": Important for Dry Stack Retaining Walls

A dry stone retaining wall is battered back to counter the force of the earth behind it. Because the wall gets narrower as it goes up, you should make the base wide. The wider the base, the more stable.

Unlike most mortared walls, which are upright and vertical, most dry stack retaining walls are built with a slight tilt back against the hill. This is called "batter" and it prevents the soil pressure behind the wall from pushing the stones out over time. A battered stone wall is a counterforce to a steep hillside. A standard is about 2–3" back for every one foot of height, depending on the slope. You can do this by stacking each successive stone layer back by about 1–1 ½". For walls that are 3' tall, the tilt back is at least 6" into the soil. Make the footing base about one-and-a-half times wider than the desired width at the top.

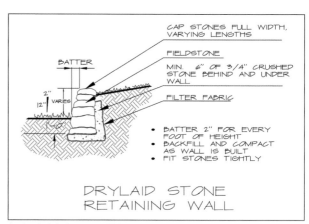

A dry laid stone wall built with a batter back into a slope.

Mortared Stone Walls: Strong, Sturdy and Everywhere

A mortared stone wall is made up of stones, cut or rough, that are bound together with a bonding agent. This is the most common method of building a wall, and for good reason: you cannot beat a mortared stone wall for strength! Mortar, a flexible filler and adhesive, stabilizes the stones and is especially useful if the wall will be used for any load-bearing tasks, such as a garden seat or retaining a slope. The benefit of a mortared wall is that it can be built with round or angular stones and is fairly maintenance-free. It also does not have any open spaces, so no small animals or snakes can take up residence here.

This lovely, rustic mortared wall is made up of local stones and is a compelling mosaic of various colored stones separated by wide mortar joints.

A mortared stone wall. The mortar between the stones is flush with the wall surface to create a smooth and more formal look. The hydrangeas are the show in the summer but the wall holds its own for the rest of the year.

It's all About the Base

A mortared wall, most importantly, needs a stable, frost-proof footing to prevent the stones from shifting. This means that, before building the wall, you must construct a foundation that extends down to the frost line in your zone. If you live in colder regions, a foundation should be as deep as 3-1/2–4' below ground level. Local building codes dictate depths of footings, height of walls and specifications for concrete footings for mortared walls. Many codes require you to insert reinforcing steel rods in a concrete foundation. It is imperative that you check these regulations before you build! Do not build a mortared wall on a shallow footing; that is courting disaster, as the wall is only as good as its base.

The Color of Mortar

Mortar is a mixture of Portland cement, hydrated lime and masonry sand. It has a creamy consistency like pancake batter and makes a great adhesive for stone – thin enough to spread easily, but stiff enough to hold its shape. You can buy mortar mix in a premixed bagged form that only requires the addition of water. There are several types of mortar mixes to choose from, so ask local masons in your area for their recommendation. Please note that mortar is not concrete and should not be interchanged with it.

Wide-jointed walls show off mortar more than any kind of wall. These stone walls, with mortar flush with the surface of the stone, can be seen in historic situations where farmers, rather than skilled masons, were the builders. The stones are not carefully fitted but spaced far apart with mortar filling the gaps. These joints may be 1" wide and can make up almost one fifth of the wall's surface.

With this much area, the color of the mortar in a wide-jointed wall is an important consideration.

The color of mortar (and how it is applied) can really affect the look of a wall, as shown here. The photo on the left is at Theodore Roosevelt's estate, Sagamore Hill, in Oyster Bay, New York. It is a historic mortar color with intentional heavy texturing. The other photo shows how cream-colored mortar enhances the pinkish color of stones.

The sand-based mortar in this wall can be seen in the Japanese Bonsai Garden at The Huntington in San Marino, California. The gray stone arrangement and the mortar shows off the Japanese tradition of excellent craftsmanship.

include buffs, tans and pink shades. The lighter colors show off the stones and can make a stone wall appear as a multi-color mosaic. Darker mortar colors make a wall more subdued, making a good backdrop.

You can go to mortar pigment websites and look at mortar colors, but shades and hues can vary, depending on screen settings. When planning a wall, it is wise to consult a physical color card (available at dealers) for a better indication of potential color. Better yet, make a few test samples of the mortar on a board to make sure that you have the desired color. Note: always allow the mortar sample to dry before you decide, as mortar lightens considerably when it is dry.

In the past, the color of mortar was primarily determined by the color of the sand and cement, but now there are powdered pigments available commercially that are specifically formulated for mixing in mortar. In fact, there are over 60 shades of color to choose from to enhance the appearance of a mortared stone wall. Popular mortar pigments

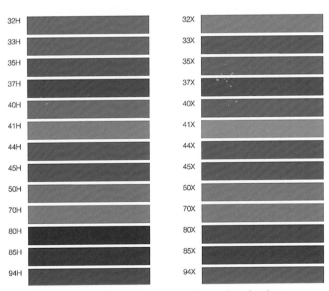

The above is a small sample of a mortar color chart from Solomon Colors (solomoncolors.com).

The Appeal of Walls With Recessed Mortar Joints

A popular style of stone wall, known as a recessed mortar wall, looks like a dry stack wall but is actually mortared. This style has joints that are filled with mortar recessed back approximately 1/2" from the face of the stone. The stone in the wall appears to have more depth and produces evident "shadow lines." For best visual effect, use a mortar that's pigmented a dark gray. The look of a recessed mortar wall can be suitable for modern as well as rustic settings.

Walls with mortar recessed in the joints between the stones look like dry stone walls but have the strength of mortared walls. This wall is in the Desert Botanical Garden in Phoenix, Arizona.

This low stone wall is in the front of my house. We built it with recessed joints to show off the stones but at the top the mortar is flush with the stones for strength and as an impervious surface. Bluestone pavers form a narrow walk next to the wall.

I often use low recessed stone walls in my landscape projects. I like them because the stones look like individual units in a wall mosaic. The joints seem as dark lines that surround each rock. It works best if the stones are a tight fit and the joints are fairly consistent in width. That way, the recessed stones provide a "reveal" that highlights the individual stones.

The corners of a recessed mortar wall can be beautifully done, as shown here. The care in its construction is clear. This wall abuts my driveway.

Rounded stones are mortared together to appear as a pile of stones at the base of large columns in the Disney Grand Californian Hotel in Anaheim, California. This hotel was designed in the rustic stone-and-timber style of the grand national park lodges, reminiscent of the Ahwahnee hotel at Yosemite National Park.

Here is an unusual example of recessed mortar! The large round rocks in the photo appear as a pile at the base of a massive building column. In reality, they are mortared together securely. This rustic use of stones harks back to the American Arts and Crafts style that celebrated natural materials and their use by artisans in architecture and gardens. This impressive stone column is at the Disney Grand Californian Hotel in Anaheim, California.

The Uses of Stone Walls in a Landscape

Stone walls shape the permanent framework of a landscape; everything else revolves around them. They separate and define areas, screen, enclose, act as a boundary marker or lead the eye. They also act as a "sheltering wall," protecting from cold and hot winds. A stone wall can stand alone as a design feature or act as a magnificent backdrop for anything set in front of it. This photo was taken at Sleepy Cat Farm in Greenwich, Connecticut.

Sheltering Walls

Smart gardeners prize stone walls on the north and west of their gardens because they face the noon and afternoon sun. The stones in the wall absorb the heat on sunny days and slowly radiate it back to the plants in cool evenings. They also protect from westerly winds.

Walled-in gardens use tall stone walls to mute noise, screen neighbors and act as backdrops for espaliered fruit trees. These quiet courtyard spaces use stone and greenery together to create a serene retreat. There is nothing as enjoyable as sitting in a walled garden amidst fragrant plants and chirping birds. The stone walls add to the enchantment.

This stone wall, lined with colorful perennials, acts as a divider between a yard and the surrounding woods.

Freestanding Stone Walls

Freestanding stone walls are called double-faced, because they are open on both sides. They stand alone and do not retain any earth. These walls can be built as dry stack or mortared. They can be loose and rustic or fitted and stately. Of course, they take more time to build, because both sides of the wall are visible. Just remember, if your wall is meant to be used as a sitting wall, then it will be load bearing and should be mortared and built to withstand pressure.

These double-faced walls can be any height and act as separators in the landscape, dividing a front yard from a street, a garden from a drive. A freestanding wall becomes a stone seam between two adjacent areas. You can build a loose dry stack wall to divide an outdoor sitting area from a planted area, and it will become an integral part of the landscape uniting and dividing at the same time. This is the beauty of a freestanding wall.

Freestanding walls serve as a visual boundary without making you feel penned in. A great backdrop for flowers, as shown here.

Like walkways, freestanding walls form strong lines in a garden that lead the eye. This photo illustrates the contrast between the soft roses and the stone wall.

Sitting Walls

Architect Christopher Alexander and associates described the benefits of a low wall perfectly in the book, *A Pattern Language*, under the section called "Sitting Wall":

SITTING WALL

This illustrates how a low wall can separate and connect at the same time, acting as an "ambiguous boundary."

A low wall ..., just at the right height for sitting, is perfect. It creates a barrier which separates. But because it invites people to sit on it – invites them to sit first with their legs on one side, then with their legs on top, then to swivel round still further to the other side, or to sit astride it – it also functions as a seam, which makes a positive connection between the two places.

A Freestanding Stone Sitting Wall

A low, freestanding stone wall can serve as a sitting wall, a perfect addition to any garden. Stone sitting walls act as a minor boundary and, because they are low enough to sit on, they also invite us to enjoy a sweet sitting spot. The wall should be mortared, no higher than 20" high and capped with smooth, relatively uniform stones for comfort.

If placed in an area with dappled light and a nice view, a stone sitting wall can be a great place for daydreaming or visiting with a friend.

I designed this stone sitting wall as a place to pause in a lovely landscape. The rounded shapes and soft flowers complement the hard stone, offering contrast and interest. The curved capstones reinforce the line of the curved paving stones. Behind the wall is a steep slope, so this sitting wall also acts as a safety barrier. It has proved to be a very popular place to sit.

A curved stone wall, capped with a wide bluestone cap, is such an inviting place! People love to sit here, talk and enjoy the flowers. Circles draw us together.

Walls can be art pieces unto themselves, acting as stone murals. The arrangement of the stone will be on view for years to come. Here the retaining wall is bordered by boxwood.

Stone Retaining Walls

Retaining walls sculpt the earth by holding back hilly terrain. They create level outdoor spaces, following the ancient farming technique of terracing. Farmers construct stone retaining walls, with one side visible, to make level cropland or terraces. Terracing in the home landscape serves a similar purpose but, in this case, they may act as a backdrop to a gracious patio or productive vegetable garden.

Determining where to place a stone retaining wall is not a quick decision. First, walk the land and consider the terrain carefully. Think where you want to create a special level area, a secluded corner or a protected site. Retaining walls, if located correctly, can be sheltering, helping to form an outdoor room to give a bit of quiet refuge.

Retaining walls also aid in controlling water runoff down a hill. They intercept water and can divert it away. By installing subsurface pipes (encased in gravel) behind a wall or using one of the drainage products designed for this purpose, you can effectively manage where to direct water. The inventive design of retaining walls can solve drainage issues and create a level, usable area at the same time.

In addition to location, consider how high to make the wall. Most municipalities require a building permit and a design from a licensed professional if your wall is taller than 4' (measured from the bottom of the first stone to the top).

Retaining walls should not be so high that they overwhelm the space they border. Look at the proportion of the height of the wall to the level land it abuts: the wall height should be substantially less than dimension of the area it abuts. For example, a 10'-wide patio can look good with a 2' retaining wall, but a higher wall may be overbearing. And, again, always make sure you have a licensed professional design the wall and construction details for a wall 4' tall and higher.

The most important aspect of retaining walls is their stability. Strong, deep foundations and adequate drainage are essential. There is no corner-cutting when it comes to building a retaining wall, so do not skimp on its construction. A poorly built wall can lean, separate or even topple over! Dig below the frost line in your area and follow the recommendations for reinforced concrete footings that are given in masonry books, websites or by your engineer.

And don't forget to provide for drainage, such as a perforated pipe encased in gravel surrounded by porous filter fabric (this prevents soil from clogging up the gravel) behind a wall. Water can

A retaining wall made of large stones to hold back a hill. Make sure you engage the services of a licensed professional for a retaining wall with a slope atop it, as shown. The trees in front will eventually grow wider, hiding the hill behind, but will not cover the wall.

weaken a retaining wall by building up behind it and applying incredible pressure. This will result in a wall bulging and leaning forward. But gravel behind the wall will direct the water to the perforated drain pipe, which collects it and then leads it out to an appropriate outlet. In short, well-built walls are constructed with drainage behind them to provide a speedy exit route for water.

Lastly, fill behind the wall with sandy or gravelly material and fully compact it. This is important because compaction directs the pressure of the fill downward rather than pushing against the wall. Here's how to do it: add several inches of gravelly fill and compact it with a vibrating tamper from a rental yard. Add several more inches, then repeat. Never backfill with topsoil and compact it; this breaks it down and the soil will collect water.

Will there be a slope behind and above the retaining wall?

Any retaining wall with a slope atop it requires the assistance of a licensed professional to design it. They will evaluate the load that will be placed on the retaining wall and determine if a design is necessary. This is critical because gravity, along with the slope, directs most of the weight of the hill toward the lower part of the retaining wall. Since soil can be heavy, you need large boulders or sturdy stone to counteract the pressure. Therefore, when it comes to retaining walls, always consult a licensed professional for advice before building.

Retaining Walls – Follow the Regulations

Most municipalities require that a licensed professional be involved in designing of retaining walls. Make sure you know your local regulations – and follow them – before building a retaining wall.

But in the end, the appearance of the stone wall is all-important. After all, this is a permanent addition to a landscape, and you may be looking at this wall for many years to come. For that reason, look at the various walls in your neighborhood. Find one you like and take a photo of it to show the mason. Also, go to the local stoneyard and see the stones that are available for your wall. They may have a wall display you can refer to. Choose stones that fit the look you want and are not too small for the mass of the wall. Many small stones in a tall retaining wall look busy and out of place.

Cap Off Your Wall In Style

Stone wall caps are cut stone pieces that span the top of a wall. They provide protection from water seeping in and make a wall suitable to sit on. Stone caps add a finished look to any wall. The details of the cap you choose can make all the difference in how the wall appears. For example, capping a wall with smooth bullnose-edged stones that overhang the wall on both sides injects a formality into a landscape. The choices can be a little daunting, so on the next page I list five considerations you face when choosing a stone wall cap.

A retaining wall with a stone cap and a rock face edge. The evergreen arborvitae trees behind it act as a living screen. That is 'Limelight' PG hydrangea (*Hydrangea paniculata grandiflora* 'Limelight') on the left.

Type of Stone and Color A cap made from the same stone as the wall can create a seamless, cohesive look. Or you can choose a different type of stone or color to create a contrast between the cap and the wall. Stone type choices include granite, limestone, bluestone, basalt and more. You may choose a stone cap that creates a pronounced color difference: a light wall capped with a dark granite cap or a dark wall highlighted by a lighter limestone cap. The effects are striking. The choice is yours, but review the contrast with stone samples before making that decision.

Thickness of Cap The thickness of the capstones you use should be in proportion to the height and width of your wall. This is probably the most important aspect relating to capstones. Do not use a capstone that is too thin, because it looks like a weak gesture and does not add any visual bulk to the wall. Choose a capstone that is at least 2" thick or thicker. If you have a larger or taller wall, you should use a proportionately thicker cap.

Cap Overhang A capstone should overhang a wall from 1-1/2–2" on each side. The overhang directs water to fall straight down and not draw back onto the stone face of the wall, where it can introduce water into the wall's core. Some masons make a small groove under the lip that hangs over the wall to stop water from running back under the overhang. The sharp edge creates a barrier that water doesn't cross.

Edge Treatment Capstones, like stone treads that are used for steps, are available in a variety of edge finishes: unfinished saw edge, thermal, bullnose, eased edge and rock face. See page 117 for more.

Width of Stone Caps The width of the wall will determine the width of the cap. If the wall is 15" wide and you want a 1-1/2" overhang, then the capstone will be 18" wide. The length of the caps is up to you.

* * *

Once you have added a stone wall or walk or rock garden, you may think you are finished with your landscaping with stone endeavors. But I say the fun is just beginning! Now it is time to consider including a stone accent in your garden. What is that? Well, the next chapter, Stone Accents for Your Garden, answers that and will give you a few ideas. I can't wait to show you!

Seven

Stone Accents for Your Garden

⌣

When life puts rocks in your way, build something nice with them.
~ folk saying

As a college student living in Kyoto, Japan, I marveled at how artisans shaped natural stone into elegant and simple garden features. From those beginnings, I developed a true appreciation for stone accents and how they can balance and unify a design without detracting from the overall space. These artful additions do not have to be formal or large to be effective – a stone accent of any type can add interest and express your personality or sense of humor. Imagine a stone frog atop a small rock at an entry gate; it seems to say "Welcome." And a stone mushroom covered with lichen set in a plant bed can make us smile.

Perhaps best of all, a stone accent is maintenance-free. Unlike other garden art, stone can withstand all sorts of weather conditions. And it only gets better with age; once a stone accent becomes covered with lichen or moss, it imparts a quiet depth to a scene. So, consider adding a stone accent to your garden. It should be something that delights you, such as a simple rock in a plant bed, a bowl of fruit atop a wall or a stone bridge spanning a dry stream. You can even paint a rock, if you'd like.

The Simplest Stone Accent

The easiest stone accent would be a large rock or outcrop that is already in your garden. You can expose it by removing any soil that covers it. Use tools to dislodge the soil (I have used screwdrivers to get in the crevices), then wash it off and let the rock's unique texture and shape shine forth. I have done this many times and I love it, because it is something like a rocky treasure hunt. One of my favorite activities is washing off a partially covered outcrop using a directed spray nozzle on the hose and watching the water reveal hidden fissures from under a thin covering of soil.

I highlighted these two natural rounded rocks with a dwarf pine, white flowers of Angelonia and blue ground hugging sedum. The arrangement makes the stones an eye-catching accent.

A large rock outcrop covered with moss makes the best kind of stone accent – it is Nature's art on display. The best thing to do is to clear around it and let the rock shine.

The next easiest thing to do is to find a rock you like and set it in your landscape. This, too, can be fun. Looking for that particular rock may entail hiking into the woods, going to a river or just going to a stone yard. You may become a rock hound, which normally means people who search out fossils and gemstones, but I like to think of it as people who appreciate rocks for their inherent beauty. Once you find your special rock, you can set it as an accent or maybe place an assortment of stones for maximum effect.

Please Touch the Rock

Rocks offer a unique opportunity to highlight the sense of touch in a garden. Placing your hands on the natural, textured surface of a rock can subtly and physically connect you to nature. The feel of the striations, indentations and coarseness of a stone may invigorate you, while the smooth, rounded surface of a water-washed stone can be calming. And there is a wide variety of textured stones to choose from: glassy rocks, layered sedimentary rocks, glacier-marked rocks, coarse, volcanic rocks and more. So why not choose rocks for their texture and encourage visitors to your garden to touch them? The presence of textural highlights of a rock are even more intriguing if you can reach out and touch them.

Rocks acted upon by ancient glaciers 10 stories thick can look water worn. You can see the holes and grooves that the ice made with its intense pressure. Perfect for touching!

The viewing stones on display in The Huntington, in San Marino, California have a sign that says:

PLEASE TOUCH THESE STONES!
Feel free to run your hand across their surfaces.
This helps to keep them polished.

Small stones, rounded by the action of water, are irresistible – we love to touch them, play with them and stack them. The solid, rounded form is comforting in our hand. I suggest you have a few rounded rocks just sitting around your garden and see if people pick them up...I bet they will.

The advice to touch a rock is based on more than feeling a stone's surface. When we are in physical contact with stone, through our hands or feet – even when we sit on them – we absorb the grounding energy that they offer. The contact with this earthy surface focuses our energy downward, helping to anchor ourselves into the earth. These days, with all the electronic tech devices around us, a little bit of natural rock grounding goes a long way. You might even consider keeping a "touching stone" on your desk or table and picking it up every so often for the same reason.

Natural Rock Art Outdoors

Simple rock sculptures show off natural striations and shapes, conveying the quiet beauty of stone. The rustic look of natural rock can fit within any outdoor setting.

Olafur Eliasson, an Icelandic artist, works with large boulders and rocks as part of his art. At Bard College in Annandale-on-Hudson, New York, Eliasson created an artwork in 2009

Strangely-shaped rocks were carefully placed leaning against each other, to create a natural rock wall. The unusual arrangement makes it artful as well as functional. This is at Innisfree.

Olafur Eliasson placed 30 boulders in his art piece in Annandale-on-Hudson. They are on an island that you can access through a covered walk. Open to the public, it is located on the north end of Bard College campus, near the Richard B. Fisher Center for the Performing Arts.

known as "The Parliament of Reality." Part of it is a 100'-diameter manmade island paved with bluestone in a pattern based upon meridian lines and navigational charts. Thirty river-washed boulders are set to act as an outdoor seating area for people to gather. The project is inspired by the Althingi, or Icelandic Parliament, the oldest national democratic institution in the world.

Ferns grow up around the large rock dinosaur consisting of native stones in Phillis Warden's garden in Bedford Hills, New York. It is set in a woodland. Whimsy at its best!

Natural Stone Whimsy in the Garden

Rocks can be used to create whimsical garden features that light up the landscape. Why should you add a whimsical accent? Because, as Paul Klee, the 20th century German artist observed, "One eye sees, the other feels." The playful stone pieces you place in your garden appeal to that feeling part of our psyche and makes us take note in a lighthearted way. It brings everyone into the same visual joke and draws us all together.

A great illustration of a whimsical stone feature is the Stegosaurus that you can see in the woodland portion of Phillis Warden's magnificent 7-acre garden in Bedford Hills, New York. Native stones from the site were carefully assembled to emulate a dinosaur walking slowly through the forest. The use of natural stones to recreate this creature is a marvel and is the last thing you expect as you walk through the woods! Guaranteed to make you smile. The Warden garden is open several times a year to the public as part of the Garden Conservancy's Open Days Program.

Another fun example can be found in the sunny gravel garden in Chanticleer, in Wayne, Pennsylvania. As you travel the grounds, you will see a large three-cushion stone sofa and a stone armchair near a large tree. The furniture was designed by Chris Woods and Doug Randolph and is remarkably lifelike and comfortable. The stone armrests even feature a TV remote! The "Fred Flintstone living room" evokes mirth and invites you at the same time to sit and relax. The whimsical stone feature draws the eye, acts as a destination to move you through the garden and then lets you pause and enjoy the moment. It exemplifies the best of what a stone accent can do! I particularly like the details of the sofa. If you look closely you will see that the armrest is composed of natural rocks atop a carved vertical support. It is ingenious and a tribute to the innovative spirit of Chanticleer, a unique pleasure garden.

How funny is this? A stone remote control sits permanently on the armrest of the sofa. Small colored gemstones make up the buttons.

Fred Flintstone's sofa at Chanticleer invites people to sit and relax. The stone really looks like cushions which is quite a feat.

Nine Tips for Placing Stone Accents in the Landscape

Have you ever found a stone carving, unusual rock or stone lantern and thought it might look good in your garden as a focal point, but didn't know where to place it? Locating a decorative accent that enhances your landscape is not difficult if you keep a few design principles in mind. You want a stone's size, color, shape, lighting and placement to be right for the location. The great Isamu Noguchi, summed it up for us: "...it is the point of view that sanctifies; it is selection and placement that will make anything a sculpture, even an old shoe."

Here are nine tips for placing stone accents to maximize their effect in a landscape:

1: Have a backdrop

A green backdrop of evergreens or tall willowy grasses softens hard stone and sets it off. Without the backdrop of a dense shrub, an evergreen tree or verdant groundcover there is no unity — the stone sits alone and may look like it was just plopped in front of a fence or in the middle of a lawn.

2: Create a viewing spot

Place stone art strategically where it can best be seen and help direct the eye. In some gardens there may be one optimal viewpoint; in others, there may be many areas from which to view the feature. It could be at the end of a walk, at a turning point, in a corner or set in a plant bed. It can serve as a focal point from the house or front entry.

3: Elevate it

Elevate a stone feature (like this finial) to draw attention to it. This technique, used by art galleries and museums, works well in a garden too. You can use a wall, a rock or a terracotta pot turned upside down as a base. I like hiding the pot in a plant bed, surrounded by foliage, and then placing a stone accent atop it.

4: Repeat it

To make a point, repeat yourself. Evenly spaced stone accents in a row in a garden make a strong, ordered statement and unify an outdoor space. This visual cue of uniform elements in a line establishes a rhythm that ties a large space together. It can also make a small area more interesting.

6: Contrast textures or color

A smooth, white stone sculpture contrasted against a background of large, deep green leaves catches the eye due to the contrast. Small, gray stones in a dry stream also look great when large-leaved hostas drape over. It is the difference in color and textures that adds interest and calls attention to the scene.

5: Group stones in odd numbers

Groupings of stones can reflect what we find in nature. The stones should be similar in their material or shape so that they look like they belong together. A group of stones adds visual importance to an area. Place groups of stones in odd numbers like 3, 5 or 7 for a harmonious setting.

7: Surround the base of a tree

Since plants are difficult to establish at the base of a tree, stones and small boulders are a natural substitute here. A mulch of smooth, rounded river stones is both an accent and a useful ground cover. It draws the eye to the base of the tree and needs no watering!

8: Light it up

When you can, consider lighting up the stone accent. Place a "well light" fixture flush in the ground at the base of a stone feature to send a beam of light up the front. This fixture is unseen, and the uplighting technique makes a dramatic statement at night. Or, place an accent near or beneath a path light, as shown here.

9: Evaluate the location carefully

Some advice from long experience: Before you move something heavy into place, take a step back and carefully evaluate the stone piece in the context of your property. Make sure this is where you want your rock feature to be sitting. Moving a rock is hard work!

A Stone as a Bridge

A rustic stone bridge can be formed from a simple slab of uncut rock laid across a stream or dry rock channel. It connects two parts of a landscape and acts as a magnet, drawing people to it. Because of this, in my projects, I look for opportunities to place a stone footbridge whenever I can. It doesn't necessarily have to be a real crossing; sometimes I place a rock even if there is no path on the other side. A rock bridge exerts a symbolic presence as much as a useful one. This is the best aspect of a stone accent!

A bridge is a good way to transition from one kind of space into another. It says, in essence, "Now you are venturing to a different kind of place." For example, you can make one side of a rock bridge a narrow garden path and the other side an open lawn area – the two scenes joined in a connection that is dramatic and subtle at the same time.

Of course, some practical considerations should be addressed when using a rustic rock as a bridge. Make sure the rock bridge is set on a stable base of flat-topped rocks set firmly in the ground (or a low wall). Walk over it and make sure the rock crossing does not jiggle or wobble. Since there are no railings, do not set it too high above the stream or channel. This little bit of slight risk is what makes traversing a stone bridge enticing. Walking across, you have to watch where you place your feet and be "present in in the moment." You cannot stare at a cell phone and cross a narrow stone bridge at the same time.

A thin, slightly bowed natural stone makes a great rustic bridge, as shown here. I placed this across a dry stream but it is only for show. The bridge leads to a small open spot on the other side. In this instance, the bridge is more of a garden accent than anything else.

Where to Place a Rustic Stone Bridge

A stone bridge can be an outdoor sculpture of sorts. The placement and the kind of stone you choose to traverse a waterway or dry stream can become the show. You may have to look for the perfect long stone to act as your bridge, but the hunt can be fun. Once you have the stone and are

Two long natural boulders make up the bridge at Michael Steinhardt's property in Mt. Kisco, New York. The overlap of the rocks at the meeting point in the middle is long enough to make it possible for people to cross. This visual break in the bridge heightens its challenging appeal.

going to place it, consider which way the bridge will be viewed. If you approach the bridge from the side, make sure that its best qualities are seen from that vantage point. If you walk to it straight on, then the view down the length of the bridge may be most important.

A good example of creative placement of a rock footbridge can be seen in Michael Steinhardt's property in Bedford, New York. In the photo shown, the bridge is positioned straight in line with the walk so you see down its length from either entry point. The crossing is made up of two long narrow rocks with flat tops that are offset from each other so that you cross from stone to the other in the middle of the bridge. The view of the two stones is captivating.

A stone footbridge viewed from the side can be especially attractive. Diagonal views of an object allow you to see two sides of an object and make it more interesting. The Impressionist painters often used this concept in their compositions, showing houses, tables and landscapes from the diagonal perspective, with the horizon line up high – like the view you see in this photo. Try to have the walk leading to your stone bridge come from the side so that you can offer a side view. Even if people don't cross it, the view and the visual connection it forms with other parts of the garden say a lot.

Dry Stone Waterfalls

A dry waterfall can be a central feature in a garden that has no water. The stones hint at a cascade and a flowing waterway. To do this, place a group of weathered standing stones together to resemble a high waterfall. The tallest stone should have a flat face over which the invisible water cascades.

The remaining stones border a level "pool" located at the base of the waterfall stone. A few smaller stones border the stream area. I advise studying photos of natural waterfalls and cascades for ideas; or better yet, if you can, go to gardens

A dry waterfall at the Cleveland Botanic Garden illustrates how to create the look of a waterway using only stones.

This dry waterfall is set up on a slight rise so that the viewer looks uphill at it. The rock arrangement symbolizes a natural waterfall and the lower viewpoint helps to make it more dramatic.

that have dry waterfall displays such as the Japan Pavilion at Disneyworld in Florida or the Cleveland Botanic Garden.

When you get the stones the way you like them, plant around the dry waterfall with plants that normally grow by the water such as iris, sedge and ferns. For added drama, light it up from below in the evening.

Have a Seat - Make a Stone Bench

Nothing conveys strength and stability in a landscape more than a stone bench. It is perfect for a quiet meditation spot; sitting on stone "grounds' you and roots you to the earth. For this reason alone, it is a good idea to have a stone seat somewhere in your outdoor space.

You can create a bench from a single stone slab that is at least 18" wide, 2" thick or more and about 3–4' long or longer. Stone slabs are rough, rectangular stone pieces (the type of stone varies with location) that are normally cut in a quarry and available in landscape supply yards. Antique stone slabs, which can be especially beautiful, are collectors' items and may be found in architectural salvage yards. For comfort, the slab you choose should be fairly free of protrusions. The underside should also be relatively smooth in order to have better contact with the support stones.

The slab can be set on two or three sturdy stone bases that are set into the ground on concrete footings. If you use natural stones as supports, use those that have flat enough tops that they'll make good contact with the bench stone. The supports should be no more than 3' apart and wide enough to cover a good portion of the width of the slab. In other words, do not make the supports narrow. You can have the slab overhang the supports by 6–8" on the ends, depending on the thickness of the stone. Of course, it is important that the tops

Here, a stone bench is fashioned from 2 solid square-shaped stone bases and a thick, rustic slab for a seat. It has a good amount of overhang on all sides which helps with rain. Notice how the bench is level even though it is standing on sloping ground.

of the support stones be the same height for a level bench. Lay a board across the stones and place a carpenter's level on top to check for level. Often, the weight of the slab works with gravity to make it stable, but it is wise to use mortar or stone adhesive to adhere the stone bench to the supports.

The height of the finished bench can vary between 16–20". When you set the support stones in place, consider the thickness of the slab to determine the finished height. A comfortable height is about 17–18", but it is all a matter of preference.

I designed this curved stone bench based on a 10' radius. It is formed from two 3"-thick curved bluestone slabs set atop three evenly spaced fieldstone piers. The two slabs were cut by a quarry and both have a chiseled rockface edge. They meet and are mortared together atop the middle pier (you can see the thin mortar line). The bench seat overhangs the piers by 2" on all sides.

It is placed in a quiet spot and faces east. We planted around it and even under it to make the bench feel like it is tucked into a green corner. It is a sweet, permanent accent in the garden, withstanding any kind of weather!

I designed this curved stone bench as a place to sit in a sunny garden. It can be seen from inside the house and so is important both as a garden accent and as a functional seat. I planted pachysandra beneath the bench as well. The treatment of the base of a bench is often overlooked.

The Benefits of Sitting on a Stone Bench

A stone bench can be a special place for "centering," offering a feeling of quiet awareness. Sit on the bench, close your eyes and keep your bare feet on the ground in front of you. Feel the energies of the earth rise up through your feet and through your body. Open your eyes and spread your arms out to let the energy course through. Listen quietly to the sounds of nature. You have been charged with earth energy and are grounded.

What is Cast Stone?

Cast stone is a highly refined concrete product that simulates the color, texture and appearance of natural cut stone. It is made from Portland cement, sand and high quality fine stone aggregate (limestone, marble or similar). It can look and feel like real stone and is often used to create finials, planters, fountains and statues for the garden. Cast stone garden ornaments are normally much lower in price than quarried stone or natural stone.

Typical finishes include acid-etched, honed, polished and brushed. Well-made cast stone can last for a very long time and improves in appearance with decades of exposure to weathering.

This ammonite sculpture, from Campania International, was a gift from a dear friend. It looks like stone but is made in Pennsylvania from cast stone.

*   *   *

The photo of the fox shown here is especially appealing because it has a backdrop of a wall of wild plants. Rocks and stone accents show off beautifully when surrounded by lush foliage and colorful flowers – a lovely counterpoint to the solidity of rock. The next chapter offers suggestions about some plants you may consider placing near and around your stone features.

Eight

Plants and Stone

~⁀

If your garden is to have "magic" you have to take your work further and give it an extra dimension..

~ Russell Page

Russell Page, the great 20th century British garden designer, noted that, in order to create "magic" in your garden, you must "be aware of the interplay of objects." The contrast between plants and stone creates that interplay. For example, a solitary textured rock looks so much more interesting when a green, leafy plant or a fleshy, low-growing sedum is planted next to it. This is because the juxtaposition between hard and soft, light and dark, feathery and solid, produces the all-important visual counterpoint that Page deemed magic in the landscape. This chapter is intended to inspire you to combine plants with rocks, and so I have provided a few selected plant recommendations for planting around stone. You do not have to plant too many next to a rock – the magic you create can be limited to a plant or two. Certainly when it comes to planting around stone, less is more.

Red pops in the shade, especially when contrasted with green. I stay away from the color blue because it tends to recede in low light conditions. Here a group of Dragon Wing® red begonias, a form of angelwing begonia, light up a shady dry stream.

Planting Around Natural Rocks in Shade

People often think that rocks in shade are an insurmountable obstacle to gardening. But, by planting the right plants, you can make a large rock outcrop or a grouping of rocks in a shady yard stand out. The trick is to choose specific plants that like these conditions. Rocks and plants are, in fact, a natural association: plants grow at the edges of large rocks for protection from the elements and to take advantage of the ground moisture that sits beneath the stone during dry times of the year. The roots grow toward the water trapped under the rock, ensuring the plant's survival. This explains why some hardy perennials grow so well next to rocks.

Of course, you don't want the rock outcrop to be hidden by plant foliage, so choose low growing plants that are well behaved in their growth habits. They must be strong growers or self-seeders to thrive in rocky environments and be suitable for partial light conditions. Some shade plants need a moist environment, so consider their water needs before planting.

A shady, rock-strewn dry stream (I spoke about this in Chapter 3, Sustainable Stone) is a perfect setting to create your magic. The stones are a natural companion to shade-tolerant shrubs such as oakleaf hydrangeas *(Hydrangea quercifolia)*, arrowwood *(Viburnum dentatum)*, Delaware Valley white azaleas, mountain andromeda *(Pieris floribunda)*, among others. I like to plant tough perennial plants along the edges, such as 'Ice Dance' sedge, 'Chocolate' bugbane *(Actaea simplex* 'Chocolate'), assorted ferns and more. It need not be fussy. Along one very shady dry stream, I simply planted a large mass of the evergreen groundcover pachysandra, which acted as a green backdrop to the rocks. For summer color, easy care annuals such as angelwing begonias and coleus fit in nicely. Just remember to water them.

Large-leaved plants such as hosta and caladium add a bold accent, catch the eye and look especially attractive against the rocks. Variegated hosta varieties, with their vivid green and white or green and yellow leaves, brighten a shady dry stream. The important thing about keeping most plants happy in the shade is to provide them with enough water. This may mean being out there with a hose or installing a sprinkler system. Again, make sure you plant them in rich garden soil amended with compost and mulch them.

You need water to sustain plants such as the dwarf hosta shown here. Before you plant, make sure you have enough water for thirsty varieties. The yellow-leaved 'Goldmound' spirea in the upper left lights up dark rocks in partial shade conditions.

Seven Shade-Tolerant Plants to Plant Near Rocks

Lily of the Valley (Convallaria majalis)

This tough, low-growing perennial is a traditional plant for planting around rocks in shady areas. It has famously fragrant dainty flowers early

Lily of the valley is a tenacious grower, as shown here. It makes a great companion in tough rocky sites.

in the spring. The petite bell-like blooms make delightful small, scented bouquets. It persists for many years, spreads by underground stems and grows easily next to rocks. Their ability to tolerate harsh conditions prompted rock garden expert Reginald Farrer to remark, "The lily of the valley is the worst of all delicious weeds when it thrives."

Lily of the valley can be planted in tight spaces between rocks but can be a nuisance spreader, so keep it away from other plants. For variety, try a pink lily of the valley (*Convallaria majalis* var. *rosea*) or a larger-flowered variety, 'Fortin's Giant' (*Convallaria majalis* 'Fortin's Giant'). To be enjoyed to their fullest, plant lily of the valley in masses. A note: all parts of the plant are considered poisonous if ingested, so beware if you have children or pets. Grows in Zones 3 through 7. This is a cool weather perennial and will perform poorly south of Zone 7a.

Bigroot Geranium (Geranium macrorrhizum)

Hardy geraniums are "true" geraniums and not the tender annual plants that most people call geraniums. This perennial, also known as rock cranesbill, is a versatile groundcover that's virtually problem-free. It is drought tolerant and adaptable to many sun and shade conditions – perfect for growing around rocks. It performs well in dry shade. Rock cranesbill spreads via underground rhizomes, so do not plant it near less vigorous plants. The flowers bloom pink for about two weeks in late spring through early summer. The foliage has a sweet piney fragrance and is deer resistant. USDA Zones 4–8.

Perennial geraniums tend to spread so be careful when planting near other plants. It looks great next to rocks in a woodland garden.

The cultivar known as 'Ingwersen's Variety' (*Geranium macrorrhizum* 'Ingwersen's Variety') grows 12–18" tall and has pleasant light pink flowers in late spring. It is more drought tolerant than others in the same family. The semi-evergreen aromatic leaves of Geranium 'Ingwersen's Variety' are tinted bronze-red in fall and look wonderful around the base of rocks.

Eastern Red Columbine
(Aquilegia canadensis)

This is a beautiful native woodland wildflower that has showy, nodding red flowers with yellow centers. In spring, when it blooms, the flowers look like little hanging lanterns. Its tubular flowers attract hummingbirds. It spreads by self-seeding, so it naturalizes easily. You can find it naturally in rocky woods and on ledges. Zones 3–8.

Eastern red columbine is an erect perennial that stands up 2' tall, topped with nodding red flower. An excellent addition to a rock garden.

Bloodroot
(Sanguinaria canadensis)

Bloodroot is a stunning native wildflower that flourishes in shady woodlands in Zones 3–8. Its pure white blossoms appear for a very short time in early spring. When the flower fades, its fairly large

Rocks do much to show off the unique large leaves of bloodroot. The leaves start out as cigar-shaped and rolled up, eventually opening up to reveal pristine white flowers. A must-have for any rocky shade garden.

leaves open to reveal a unique shape that look like webbed feet. Rocks show it off to great effect.

Bloodroot will go dormant in mid-to-late summer, especially in dry soils. It grows 6" high. This perennial self-seeds and grows in colonies. You may consider the double-flowered 'Multiplex' variety.

Jack Frost Brunnera
(Brunnera macrophylla 'Jack Frost')

Rocks in shade make for a dark corner, but the shimmering silver foliage of this deer-resistant groundcover plant will brighten any scene! The broad, heart-shaped highly frosted leaves are etched by emerald-green veins that contrast vividly against gravel or dark stones. In spring, delicate sprays of small bright blue forget-me-not flowers dance above the plant.

These easy-to-grow plants slowly spread by underground rhizomes. 'Jack Frost' needs little care and attains a 12–15" height. Try another variety, 'Kings Ransom', for a leaf with a creamy yellow margin and light frosting throughout. Zones 3–8.

Ostrich fern, being tall, makes a great backdrop or can stand alone next to a raised rocky bed. The ease and versatility of ferns make them a great companion to rocks and an essential part of a shady garden.

'Jack Frost' bugloss is an eye-catcher, with its frosted leaves illuminating the garden floor. Here, I planted it amongst rocks and placed a white quartz-laden rock next to it to emphasize the white effect in the garden.

Ostrich Fern (Matteuccia struthiopteris)

Few plants are as delicate yet as durable as this large, graceful fern. It is excellent for rocky, shady gardens with rich soil and spreads slowly by underground stems. The feathery fronds reach 3' tall before gently arching over at the tips. They grow in a tropical-looking vase shape, which makes an effective counterpoint to jagged rocks. It is a charming backdrop to shorter plants in the front.

The ostrich fern is easy to grow, and deer tend to leave it alone. It likes water, so plant in a site with damp shade. They also appreciate an occasional top dressing of leaf litter or compost mulch. The delicate fronds need protection from wind damage and will turn brown in the fall. It grows best in zones 3–7.

Plants that Grow in the Cracks and Crevices of Walls and Stones

Stone walls and rocky sites that have low-growing plants popping out of the cracks and crevices are a treat in the landscape. The tiny plants are unexpected and always eye-catching. You don't often see this, because there are few plants that can tolerate the tough circumstances – little water and little soil. These particular "crevice plants" grab onto the smallest of cracks and seem to defy all odds in their precarious perch. In walls: the wall has a moderating effect on the microclimate in these pockets; the plants within are warmer and less waterlogged in the winter and cooler and moister in the summer. In rocks: the rocks help to channel rain and snowmelt water to the plants while the top dries out.

The plants that will do best are ones you see naturally growing on cliffs and ledges. Rocky sites and dry stone retaining walls, with many gaps, are the best candidates for crevice plants.

You can plant in a crevice or pocket by wedging a small pebble into the bottom of the gap to keep soil from washing out. Now press some top-quality freely draining soil into this little space. Plant very small plants – bare-root for best

The white clustered flowers of common yarrow (*Achillea millefolium*) pokes out from a space in a wall. This plant tolerates poor soils so it is suited for a natural sunny rock garden or in a stone wall. It is considered by many to be an aggressive weed but here it is contained.

results – that will send out roots to establish themselves. Do not shove established plants into the opening, because they will have a hard time adapting to the new harsh conditions. If you do not have bare root plants, then remove the plant from a small pot and carefully separate the soil from the roots, maybe even trimming them a little. Use a narrow trowel, dibble or gardening knife to guide the roots into the crevice. Fill with a small amount of loose, light soil and tamp lightly into place. Water with a dilute rooting fertilizer.

Some Recommended Plants for Crevice Planting

Choose plants that are drought tolerant, because these adapt to the dry conditions and require less watering. The plants should also be suitable for the sun and shade conditions you have – do not plant sun-loving plants in a shady wall. Lastly, do not forget to consider your hardiness zone.

Plants growing on cliff faces and in rocky crevices will usually be at home growing out of gaps in a stone wall, but consider the stone type that makes up the wall. For example, if the wall is made from limestone, or has a lime mortar mix in it, then it will be alkaline and unsuitable for acid-loving plants such as certain ferns.

Siberian Spurge
(Euphorbia Seguieriana ssp. Niciciana)

This hardy plant has needle-leafed foliage and handsome yellow flowers which bloom in late spring and last for months. It makes a tidy mound in a rock garden, growing 12–18" tall and wide. Best in full sun and well-drained soils. Easy to grow and tolerant of drought. And it is deer and rabbit resistant.

Siberian spurge

Try Sedum!

For rocks in sun, try planting sun-loving succulents such as sedum, also known as stonecrop. They are drought tolerant and take root in the tightest of places.

The green succulent leaves of stonecrop *(Sedum)* partially cover these boulder steps. Although the look is delightful, periodic cutting is necessary to keep it in check.

The genus name, Sedum, comes from the Latin *sedo*, which means to sit, because they seem to "sit" on rocks and ledges and, in time, form a low-growing mat. Many varieties bloom abundantly in spring or summer, but they are mainly grown for their foliage ranging from gray to blue to green to red tinged. Sedums can be found in all zones. Some are adapted to colder regions, while others are suited to warm and even hot, arid climates. Overwatering will impair growth.

Goldmoss Stonecrop *(Sedum acre)*

This is a perfect choice for crevices, rock gardens and stepping stones where there is little water available. It is a perennial that is covered with showy yellow flowers in spring and summer. An old time favorite, it can be one of the best naturalizing, rock crevice plants available. It can spill over retaining walls with ease and can engulf a rock garden if you are not careful. Try the golden variety, *Sedum acre* 'Aureum'. Zones 3–9.

'Weihenstephaner Gold' Stonecrop *(Sedum kamtschaticum* var. *floriferum* 'Weihenstephaner Gold')*

This dark green succulent has a dense habit and is easy to grow. Covered in clusters of canary-yellow, star-shaped flowers in late spring, it spreads slowly to form a lustrous green mat that drapes over rocks. The short-stemmed flowers turn orange with age. Attracts butterflies. Grows 4" tall. Zones 4–9.

Yellow star-shaped flowers of 'Weihenstephaner Gold' sedum drape over several sunny rocks. Easy to grow, in spring it is a show stopper and attracts butterflies to your garden.

'Vera Jameson' sedum

'Vera Jameson' Sedum
(Hylotelephium telephium subsp.
telephium 'Vera Jameson')

This sedum is a low, clump-forming succulent with rounded, smoky-blue leaves that turn deep burgundy. It is a great choice for rock gardens and for edging in sunny gardens. It grows to 9–12". tall. The dusky-pink flowers are bee and butterfly attractors and are suitable for drying. Tough and easy to grow, it loves a hot, dry location. Zones 4–9.

Hens and Chicks *(Sempervivum tectorum)*

These are small, mat-forming plants, 3–6" tall, that are grown for their hardy, succulent rosette foliage. Native to Northern Europe, they like full sun, are drought tolerant and thrive in well-drained soils. Their name comes from the offsets or chicks that cluster around the mother or hen plant. The chicks spread out, forming an ever-widening colony. They can cling to walls as shown. *Sempervivum* has a thick stalk with tubular or star-like blooms on the top. Zones 3–11.

Hens and chicks

'Blue Rose' Echeveria (Echeveria imbricata)
Also called hens and chicks, this plant is native to
Mexico and will not tolerate any frost. It has tight
rosettes of blue-green leaves that bear clusters of
red and yellow flowers on slender flower stalks
in spring and early summer. It is wonderful as a
rock garden plant, spreading slowly by offsets.
Zones 9–11. It is shown here with ice plant
(*Delosperma cooperi*).

Eastern prickly pear cactus

Eastern Prickly Pear Cactus
(*Opuntia humifusa*)

You may not expect to see cactus anywhere
outside the arid desert, but Eastern prickly pear
is a native to Eastern North America. If you have
a rock in full sun that has a freely draining large
crevice, you might try this interesting plant with
its bright yellow flowers and red edible fruits
(the prickly pears, which can be made into jellies
and pickles).

Prickly pear attracts bees and butterflies and can
be a star on any large, sunny rock outcropping. To
get it started, put on a pair of thick gloves, spread
some sand in the crevice where you want them
to grow and insert a few cactus pads, cutting-side
down. These will grow into a thick mat of bristly
cactus pads. Zones 2–10

'Blue Rose' echeveria

Yellow Plants Among the Rocks

Whenever I create a rock garden or plant around a rock outcrop I try to include some yellow in the mix. Yellow grabs the eye and contrasts vividly against the gray color of stones. But take care not to plant too much yellow, because it may overpower the scene. It is a balancing act between the vibrant yellow and the solidity of the stone. Whether you have sun or shade, you can include a yellow-flowering or yellow-leaved plant among the rocks. Here are some easy-to-grow yellow plants to consider (arranged in alphabetical order based on genus names):

'Gold Heart' bleeding heart

'All Gold' Japanese forest grass

'Gold Heart' Bleeding Heart
(*Dicentra spectabilis* 'Gold Heart')

Old-fashioned bleeding heart is a shade perennial with arching stems of heart-shaped pink flowers. The yellow variety has vivid golden foliage, perfect for shady woodland gardens hanging over rocks. Plants go dormant during the summer, so team them with plants such as hosta and hellebores. 24–36" tall. Zones 3–9

'All Gold' Japanese Forest Grass
(*Hakonechloa macra* 'All Gold')

Unlike most grasses, 'All Gold' Japanese forest grass does well in partial shade. Its narrow, bright-yellow blades are eye popping, especially among rocks. It is a short (9–15" tall) clump-forming grass that is deer resistant. It will take on a more chartreuse coloring in shade. Shown here with magenta 'Caracas' celosia, an annual. Zones 5–9

Variegated Sweet Iris *(Iris pallida* 'Variegata'*)*
The striped green and yellow sword-like leaves are
a flashy accent in a rock garden. Native to rocky
areas in northern Italy, it sports lavender-blue
bearded flowers in late spring. Best in full sun.
Once established, it is somewhat drought tolerant
and requires little maintenance. Rabbits and deer
rarely bother this plant. Perennial. Zones 4–9

Yellow oregano

Variegated sweet iris

Yellow Oregano
(Origanum vulgare 'Aureum'*)*
This is both visually appealing and a fragrant herb
but has little culinary value. Its golden-yellow
leaves fan out over rocks to create a lovely accent.
This drought tolerant perennial grows 9–18" tall
and has tiny pinkish-purple flowers. Here it is in
the background with blue lavender in front. Best
with some afternoon shade. Zones 6–8.

'Angelina' Stonecrop
(*Sedum rupestre* 'Angelina')

This popular, low growing evergreen sedum works well on a dry rock outcrop. Its needle-like foliage forms a trailing mat of succulent golden-yellow leaves. It is covered in clusters of yellow starry flowers during the summer. In winter, foliage turns orange in northern climates. Zones 3–11.

'Pineapple Splash' coleus

'Angelina' sedum

'Pineapple Splash' Coleus
(*Solenostemon scutellarioides*)

A bold, upright variety of the popular foliage plant, this coleus has stunning pineapple-colored leaves with rosy veins. It is sun tolerant and does well in hot weather. Grows 24–36" tall. Coleus leaves of lime-green, bright yellow and purple, with shades of chocolate, burgundy or red look great near rocks or stone walls. Perennial in Zone 10 and above.

Coleus 'Wasabi'

This is a vigorous upright grower (to 30" tall) known for its bright, spicy, lime-green leaves. Neat, sharp edges and color make this a popular coleus. The best color develops on plants that get at least a half-day of sunshine.

'Sweet Kate' spiderwort

'Wasabi' coleus

'Sweet Kate' or Blue & Gold Spiderwort (*Tradescantia* 'Sweet Kate')

'Sweet Kate' spiderwort is an easy-to-grow perennial that produces a profusion of deep-blue flowers from summer to fall. An eye-catching accent with vibrant golden-yellow foliage, it grows best in a partly shady site to prevent leaf burn. It slowly expands from year to year, preferring moist soil, but tolerating drought once established. When the stems of spiderworts are cut, they secrete a viscous liquid which becomes threadlike and silky upon hardening – like a spider's web; hence its common name. Zones 5–8

Cascading Plants – Drama Among the Stones

One of the most intriguing combinations is a rock or stone wall draped with a cascading plant. The trailing branches of groundcovers, shrubs and even some trees weeping over a rocky surface create an interesting scene, sometimes resembling a water cascade. If you want to try this, pick a weeping or prostrate plant that is suitable for your climate conditions and make sure you have enough soil for its roots at the top of a wall or outcrop. Try to plant close to the edge so it can fall gracefully.

Always consider its watering needs. Irrigation systems help to maintain the health of the plants. In time, the cascading plant may grow so luxuriantly that you may have to prune it to keep it from covering the stonework. Flowing plants that hang over a wall, like the vividly colored blooms of creeping phlox *(Phlox subulata)* are so satisfying when they are at their best. Here are a few suggestions for cascading plants; they illustrate how effective these types of plants can be.

Lace Shrub *(Stephanandra incisa* 'Crispa')

This deciduous shrub is a mounding, low-growing, deciduous shrub that typically grows 1–2' tall with wide–spreading, arching branches that tend to weep down. Best known for finely-cut foliage, they drape over stone walls easily. Grow in average, medium, well-drained soil in full sun to part shade. Turns yellow and orange in the fall. Zones 4–10

Lace shrub

Japanese garden juniper

Japanese Garden Juniper
(Juniperus procumbens 'Nana'*)*

The low spreading dense evergreen hugs the ground and doesn't mind slightly dry conditions, nor being near hot stones in the summer. Plant some pastel-colored blooming lantana along with it. The two create a sweet yet tough sun-loving combination. They don't mind slightly dry conditions nor being near hot stones in the summer. Zones 4–9.

'Blue Pacific' Shore Juniper
(Juniperus conferta 'Blue Pacific'*)*

This is a low, spreading juniper that has dense blue-green foliage. Heat and drought tolerant, it grows well among rocks. Full sun. Zones 5–9.

Blue Pacific shore juniper

Rocks and Moss

I end this chapter by highlighting the close collaboration between moss and stone. The association of enduring rock and ancient moss, the oldest terrestrial plant on earth, is timeless and forms a relaxing scene that is soothing to our senses. If nothing else, if you have rocks and some water, you can grow one of the many varieties of moss. In fact, you can paint quite a display with these native, shade tolerant plants in various colors and textures.

Moss, a bryophyte, does not produce pollen, seeds or flowers, and it does not feed on anything that it is attached to. Moss obtains all its nutrients from rainfall and sunlight. It works to create soil, which is so necessary, but it does more than that. It is said that mosses collectively provide more carbon offset than all the trees in the world. And what is more, mosses have impressive water-holding potential, with a number of species able to hold 20 or more times their own weight in water. Talk about keeping rainwater on site! So, consider encouraging moss to grow on your stone pathways, retaining walls and accent rocks. They will sing to you in calming tones. There is a place for moss and rocks in any shady garden.

Moss grows naturally on rocks and steps to create a verdant, soft covering. These gardens would not be as sweet without the moss. And it holds excess water and starts the soil building process – both sustainable and beautiful.

Nine

In Closing

The simplest things in life are the most extraordinary.
~ Paulo Coelho

This book celebrates rocks in the landscape. A natural material, wrested from the recesses of the earth, rocks are often overlooked in favor of plants. But once we stop and look, we may appreciate their unique and versatile qualities. First, we see their shape and texture and any encrusted microcrystals that glint in the sun.

Next, we value their use in walks, steps, walls, and as artful accents. Finally, we see how rocks are the truest expression of a place and recognize the quiet vitality they exude. Far from being inert, rocks can be a powerful presence in a landscape. As the contemporary artist Andy Goldsworthy says, "You must smell the rocks."

My love of stone led me to work with rocks; many of the photos in this book are from landscapes I have created. As I set them in a rock garden, along dry streams or as standing stones, I enjoy a kind of "rock awareness." I silently talk to the stones as I work with them. The operative word here is "silently" because if I did this out loud people around me would wonder what I was doing. Nonetheless, I do talk to the rocks. And surprisingly, the rocks respond and let me know if they are amenable to change – or not. These rock conversations can be enjoyed by anyone. You just have to listen.

It is the same with those small pebbles that we often collect and drop into our pocket. I have a friend who collects a rock from wherever she goes. Naturally, her rock collection is immense and the butt of family jokes. But you may understand her penchant for stones. This predilection is best described by John Lame Deer, in his book, *Lame Deer: Seeker of Visions*:

You are always picking up odd-shaped stones, pebbles and fossils,
saying that you do this because it pleases you, but I know better.
Deep inside you there must be an awareness of the rock power,
of the spirits in them,
otherwise you would not pick them up and fondle them as you do.

How true. It is the rock power that you feel in a stony place. If you pick a pebble up and carry it with you, then you have a little bit of that place with you. That influence extends to all things built with stone, such as walls and steps – they add an authenticity that man-made materials just can't.

We co-create with stone. It is a collaboration between man and rock. You could say using rocks in our surroundings is our grateful nod to a bountiful Mother Earth. And that is good. As Douglas Wood notes in his book, *Grandad's Prayers of the Earth*:

"Rocks pray too," said Grandad. "Pebbles and boulders and old weathered hills. They are still and silent, and those are two important ways to pray." ∽

Places to Visit

These selected gardens, and other venues, are open to the public. They each have some sort of stonework or rock garden features that are worthy of a visit. There are many others that are not listed and I hope you add their names to this list as you travel. Rock on!

Anderson Japanese Garden, Rockford, Illinois
http://www.andersongardens.org/

Andreas Canyon Trail, Palm Springs, California
www.trails.com

Bellevue Botanical Garden, Bellevue, Washington
www.bellevuebotanical.org

Bloedel Reserve, Bainbridge Island, Washington
www.bloedelreserve.org

Brooklyn Botanic Garden, Brooklyn, New York
www.bbg.org

Chanticleer Garden, Wayne, Pennsylvania
www.chanticleergarden.org

Cleveland Botanic Garden, Cleveland, Ohio
www.cbgarden.org

Coastal Maine Botanic Gardens,
Boothbay, Maine
www.mainegardens.org

Chicago Botanical Garden, Glencoe, Illinois
http://www.chicagobotanic.org

Dallas Arboretum and Botanical Gardens,
East Dallas, Texas
www.dallasarboretum.org

Denver Botanical Garden, Alpine Rock Garden,
Colorado
www.botanicgardens.org

Desert Botanical Garden, Phoenix, Arizona
www.dbg.org

J. Paul Getty Center, Los Angeles, California
www.getty.edu/museum

Golden Gate Park, San Francisco, California –
the Japanese Tea Garden
https://goldengatepark.com/
japanese-tea-garden.html

Hamilton Gardens, Waikato, New Zealand
www.hamiltongardens.co.nz

The Huntington Library, Art Collections and
Botanical Gardens, in San Marino, California
www.huntington.org

Innisfree, Millbrook, New York
www.innisfreegarden.org

Japanese Friendship Garden, San Diego, California
www.niwa.org

Lotusland, Montecito, California
www.lotusland.org *(go here for reservations)*

Missouri Botanical Garden, St. Louis, Missouri
www.missouribotanicalgarden.org

Morikami Museum, Delray Beach, Florida
http://morikami.org/

The Mount, Lenox, Massachusetts
www.edithwharton.org

New York Botanical Garden, Bronx, New York – the
Native Garden
NYBG.org

Opus 40, Saugerties, NY
www.opus40.org

Phipps Conservatory and Botanical Gardens,
Center for Sustainable Landscapes, Pittsburgh,
Pennsylvania
www.phipps.conservatory.org

Portland Japanese Garden, Portland, Oregon
http://japanesegarden.com/

JC Raulston Arboretum, North Carolina State
University, Raleigh, North Carolina
https://jcra.ncsu.edu

Rock of Ages Visitors Center, Barre, Vermont
www.rockofages.com/en/visitors/overview/

United States Botanic Garden, Washington, D.C.
www.usbg.gov

Wave Hill, Bronx, New York
https://www.wavehill.org

Bibliography and Books of Interest

Below is a list of the books that I have quoted from in The Spirit of Stone and also some wonderful books about natural stone in the landscape and masonry that I think you will enjoy.

Adams, Henry S. *Making a Rock Garden* New York: Mcbride, Nast & Company. 1912.

Alexander, Christopher et al. *A Pattern Language: Towns, Buildings, Construction* New York: Oxford University Press. 1977.

_____, *The Timeless Way of Building* New York: Oxford University Press. 1977.

Chatto, Beth *Drought-Resistant Planting: Lessons From Beth Chatto's Gravel Garden* London: Frances Lincoln. Reprint edition 2016.

Eiseley, Loren *All the Strange Hours: The Excavation of a Life* Lincoln, Nebraska: Bison Books. 2000.

Eiseley, Loren *The Firmament of Time* Lincoln, Nebraska: Bison Books 1999.

Erdoes, Richard and Lame Deer *John Lame Deer, Seeker of Visions* New York: Simon & Schuster. 1994.

Field, Curtis *The Forgotten Art of Building a Stone Wall* Dublin, New Hampshire: Yankee Magazine. 1965.

Goldsworthy, Andy *Stone* New York: Harry N. Abrams. 1994.

Grese, Robert *Jens Jensen: Maker of Natural Parks and Gardens* Baltimore: Johns Hopkins University Press. 1998

Hu, Kemin, Elias, Thomas and Singer, Jonathan M., photographer *Spirit Stones: The Ancient Art of the Scholars' Rock* New York: Abbeville Press. 2014.

Jellicoe, Geoffrey, Jellicoe, Susan, Goode, Patrick and Lancaster, Michael *The Oxford Companion to Gardens, new edition* New York: Oxford University Press. 1991.

Pleasant, Barbara and Kane, Dency, photographer *Garden Stone – Creative Ideas, Practical Projects, and Inspiration for Purely Decorative Uses* Massachusetts: Storey Books. 2002.

Rocherelle, Gayatri Carole, and Richard Felber, photographer *The Landscape Diaries: Garden of Obsession* New York: Ruder-Finn Press. 2007.

Saito, Katuso and Wada, Sadaji *Magic of Trees and Stones: Secrets of Japanese Gardening* Tokyo: Japan Publications Trading Co. 1965.

Takei, Jiro and Keane, Marc P. *Sakuteiki: Visions of the Japanese Garden: A Modern Translation of Japan's Gardening Classic* (Tuttle Classics) Vermont: Tuttle Publishing. 2008.

Thomas, R. William *The Art of Gardening: Design Inspiration and Innovative Planting Techniques from Chanticleer* Portland, Oregon: Timber Press. 2015.

Wood, Douglas and Lynch, P.J. *Granddad's Prayers of the Earth* Massachusetts: Candlewick Press. Reprint edition 2009.

Index

Index

Index

Acknowledgments

Every book has its nugget of a beginning. That happened when Paul Kelly, publisher of St. Lynn's Press, perceived my penchant for rocks and suggested I write a book about stone in the garden. It was one of those "lightbulb" moments and I want to thank Paul for getting me started on this labor of love.

Another guiding light was Jim Peterson, publisher of *Garden Design* magazine. He probably didn't know it but his infectious enthusiasm for promoting garden design ideas served as a model for my research, photos and writing.

I would also like to thank all my friends and family for being patient with my absences. Writing a book requires a lot of "alone time" and I want to especially thank my husband, Rafael Algarin, for his quiet perseverance as I toiled away month after month on yet another extracurricular endeavor. I am very lucky to have such wonderful people in my life.

I also must strongly thank my associate, Laura McKillop, for being my primary sounding board and chief reviewer. She was with me from the very beginning when I was outlining what a book on stone in the garden might look like. From those early days to the final edits, Laura, an avid garden book collector and reader, has been there to observe, opine and also create all the drawings and diagrams in this book. I cannot express how grateful I am for her support. Thank you, Laura!

And of course, I am grateful to my editor, Cathy Dees, a fellow traveler whose keen intellect and sharp eye kept my text concise and my thoughts organized. She was everything a writer needs – offering wisdom, guidance and friendship. And thanks also to my art director, Holly Rosborough, a creative soul who has made this book the visual gem that I hoped it would be.

And thank you to my wonderful clients for allowing me to share photos of their properties! Without the photos of their stones, rock gardens, walls, steps and more, this book would not have been the same. So a big thanks goes out to Marc and Rosemary, Edward and Maya, Ted and Mary Jo, David and Melanie, Paul and Kim, Tom and Cindy, Jeffrey and Joanne, Michael and Laura, Jeff and Andrea, Paul and Jennifer, Tom and Maureen, Richard and Linda, Mark and my other clients, whom I admire very much. ∽

About the Author

Designer and author Jan Johnsen was introduced to the sublime beauty of natural stone in the landscape as a young professional living in Kyoto, Japan, and working for a landscape architecture firm. She has been active in horticulture and landscape design for over 40 years. She studied landscape architecture at the University of Hawaii and got her on-the-ground horticultural training from a Versailles-trained French gardener at Mohonk Mountain House in New York. She taught at Columbia University for seven years, is an award-winning instructor at the New York Botanical Garden, and is co-principal, with her husband, of Johnsen Landscapes & Pools, located in Westchester County, NY (www.johnsenlandscapes.com).

Jan loves to write about gardens and garden design. *The Spirit of Stone* is her fourth book, her most recent being *Heaven is a Garden* (St. Lynn's Press, 2014). She shares her passion for stone and its use in the garden at The Spirit of Stone on Facebook (www.facebook.com/thespiritofstone) and on her popular blog, Serenity in the Garden (www.serenityinthegarden.blogspot.com).

OTHER BOOKS FROM ST. LYNN'S PRESS

www.stlynnspress.com

Heaven is a Garden
by Jan Johnsen
160 pages • Hardback
ISBN: 978-0-9855622-9-8

The Cocktail Hour Garden
by C.L. Fornari
192 pages • Hardback
ISBN: 978-0-9892688-0-6

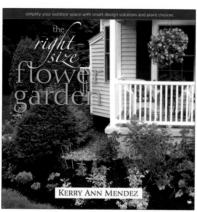

The Right-Size Flower Garden
by Kerry Ann Mendez
192 pages • Hardback
ISBN: 978-0-9892688-7-5

Yards
by Billy Goodnick
160 pages • Hardback
ISBN: 978-0-9855622-1-2